CRICUT EXPLORE AIR 2

A Complete Practical DIY Guide to Master your Cricut Explore Air 2 and Start a Profitable Business with your Machine. Tips and Tricks Included

Kimberly Johnson

Table of Contents

INTRODUCTION

The possibilities are limitless with the Cricut Explore Air 2, Cricut's fastest ever cutting machine, ready to create personalized, professional-looking DIY projects. Cut, write and score incredible designs quicker than ever. Two times faster than the Explore Air, this machine cuts over 100 materials, from paper and cardstock to vellum and leather.

Cricut Explore's Smart Set dial is a material selection dial that offers pre-defined settings to get the best results on paper, vinyl, iron-on, cardstock, fabric, poster board, and more. The Smart Set dial eliminates the need to make manual pressure, depth, and speed adjustments. All you need to do is turn the dial to your material type and press the Go button!

Cut and write up to 2X faster than previous Cricut Explore models with this DIY speed machine. The Cricut Explore Air™ 2 cuts over 100 materials everything from cardstock, vinyl, and iron-on to specialty materials like glitter paper, cork, and bonded fabric. Quickly. Beautifully. From cards to custom T-shirts to home decor, Cricut makes it easy to realize your creative vision. Design on the go on your laptop, iPad, or iPhone. Browse and play with thousands of images, fonts, and ready-to-make projects. Or create your design from scratch. The machine's Smart Set dial and custom material selection in the Design Space app puts more than 100 different material settings at your fingertips.

Pack Size: 61 x 24.1 x 24.1cm (24 x 9.5 x 9.5 inches)

Includes Cricut Explore Air 2 machine, built-in Bluetooth, Design Space software and app, German carbide premium blade, USB cord and power cord, accessory adapter, 100+ free images, 50+ free project ideas, a guide to getting started, a pen and cardstock sample and a 12 x 12-inch LightGrip cutting mat

- Mint color model
- Up to two times faster than the Explore Air
- Use Design Space app to create with PC, Mac, iOS, and Android devices
- New iOS offline mode
- Upload your own images for free (.svg, .jpg, .png, .bmp, .gif, .dxf)
- Embedded Bluetooth for wireless cutting
- Flexible and easy to use
- Cuts more than 100 materials including paper, card, vellum, leather, and more
- Smart Set dial for easy material settings
- Dual carriage for cutting and writing or cutting and scoring in one simple step
- Works with Cricut cartridges
- Cuts printable images
- Features integrated storage compartments

CHAPTER 1: WHAT IS CRICUT EXPLORE AIR 2?

For beginners, the Cricut Explore Air 2 is a cutting machine that utilizes smart technology. It cuts and writes up to 2x faster than previous models. The Cricut Explore Air 2 cuts over 100 materials. It can cut everything from cardstock, vinyl, and iron-on to thick materials like leather. The Cut Smart technology allows you to precisely cut a wide variety of materials with incredible precision.

The Cricut Explore Air 2 also offers wireless cutting, writing, and scoring with built-in Bluetooth. This wireless technology allows you to cut intricate details with ultimate precision to create stunning stationery and dazzling decor details. As well as this, you'll be able to use Cricut Pens to make handwritten-style cards and projects, with over 370 fonts to choose from, or use a favorite font from your computer for free! Additionally, with the Scoring Stylus, you can create perfect fold lines for cards, envelopes, boxes, 3D papercrafts, acetate pinwheels, and much more.

The Cricut Explore Air 2 is the easiest, fastest way to turn your creative ideas from your imagination into a reality! Choose from a range of more than 60,000 images in the Cricut image library, design on your PC, Mac, iOS, or Android device through Design Space – a free, cloud-based software – or create and upload your own (as .svg, .jpg, .bmp, .gif or .dxf files). You'll be able to transform your designs into everything from home decor and handmade cards to gifts, fashion, and more. Designing with your computer, iPad, and iPhone has never been easier and the Cricut Explore Air 2 allows you to get creative on-the-go. Design anytime, anywhere. There is also a new offline feature to try, allowing you to design without an Internet connection.

Features

Feature	Explore One	Explore Air	Explore Air 2	Maker

Easy enough for anyone to master	✔	✔	✔	✔
Cuts, writes, and scores 100 popular craft materials	✔	✔	✔	✔
Bluetooth® wireless technology		✔	✔	✔
Double tool holder		✔	✔	✔
Up to 2X faster cutting and writing			✔	✔
10X more power to cut hundreds of more materials				✔
Rotary Blade for fabrics				✔
Knife Blade* for thicker materials				✔
Scoring Wheel* tools for razor-sharp folds				✔

** Sold Separately.*

- ❖ This DIY speed machine combines time-saving performance and class-leading simplicity
- ❖ Cuts 100 materials – everything from cardstock, vinyl, and iron-on to a range of specialty materials
- ❖ Fine-Point Blade for cutting a wide variety of popular craft materials
- ❖ Fast Mode for up to 2X faster cutting and writing
- ❖ Bluetooth wireless technology

- Compatible with Scoring Stylus and Deep-Point Blade (sold separately)
- Double tool holder to keep blade and pen always at the ready
- Design Space software for iOS, Android, Windows, and Mac
- Upload and use your images and fonts for free
- Compatible with Cricut cartridges

Compared to previous models using Fast Mode, which works with popular materials including vinyl, iron-on, and cardstock. Now it's faster and easier than ever to create personalized, professional-looking DIY projects with the Cricut Explore Air 2 Machine-Mint. It's the fastest cutting machine and can cut over 100 materials from paper to leather for a wide range of projects from cards and custom t-shirts to home decor. Flexible and easy-to-use, this machine can be also used when on the go.

- Up to two times faster than Explore Air. Adjustable cutting and writing speed up to 2x faster. Up to two times faster than Explore Air.
- Design Space App for PC, Mac iOS devices (Android coming soon)
- New iOS offline mode
- Flexible and easy to use.
- Cuts more than 100 materials.
- Quick Projects. Choose to Make It Now projects or make quick cuts with the Cricut Design Space app.
- Design on-the-go. Create on your computer, tablet, or smartphone
- Embedded Bluetooth for wireless cutting
- Dual carriage for cutting and writing or cutting and scoring in one simple step

- Upload your own images for free (.svg, .jpg, .png, .bmp, .gif, .dxf)
- Cut materials from vellum to leather
- Smart Set dial for easy material settings
- Cut Smart precision cutting
- Works with Cricut cartridges
- Cuts printable images
- Integrated storage compartments

CRICUT COMPARISON

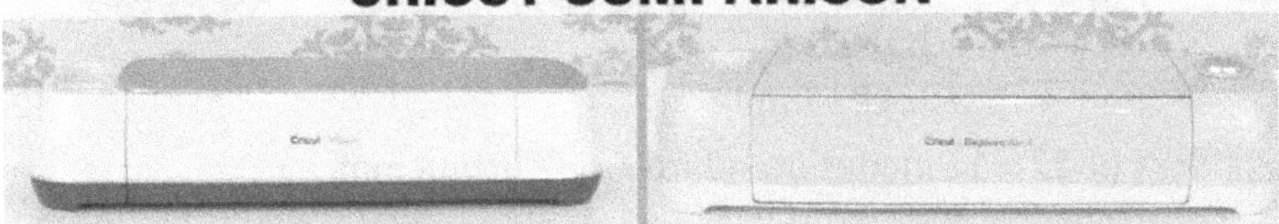

MAKER	EXPLORE AIR 2
Bluetooth for wireless cutting	Bluetooth for wireless cutting
Rotary blade for cutting fabric stabilizer free	Can use cartridges
Knife blade for cutting thick Materials	Smart dial for easy material settings
2x Fast mode for cutting & writing	2x fast mode for cutting & writing
Can upload own images for free	Can upload own images for free
Design software for PC, Mac & iOS Mobile	Design software for PC, Mac & iOS Mobile

Included In The Box:

- Cricut Explore Air 2 Machine
- Built-in wireless Bluetooth
- Cricut Design Space software & app
- German carbide premium blade
- USB cord and power cord
- Accessory Adapter
- 100+ free images
- 50+ free project ideas
- Getting started guide
- Pen & cardstock sample
- Cut 12 x 12 inches Standard Grip cutting mat
- Premium Fine-Point Blade + Housing
- Fine Point Pen, Black
- LightGrip Mat, 12" x 12" (30.5 cm x 30.5 cm)

1. Cut

Cut intricate details with ultimate precision, from lace stationery designs to fine snowflakes and spider webs for holiday décor.

2. Score

Make a beautiful, handcrafted card with a complimentary envelope in minutes. Scoring Stylus makes easy-to-fold creases in the most popular paper materials with Cricut machines.

3. Write

Cricut machines handle pens like your very own calligrapher, embellishing projects with beautiful text and delicately drawn shapes. With a variety of styles and thicknesses, Cricut pens simply make your projects stand out.

4. Cut 100+ Different Materials

Cricut Explore machines cut a hundred different materials – everything from the most popular craft materials like cardstock, vinyl, and iron-on to specialty materials like glittery paper, polished foils, and bonded fabric. The Smart Set dial and custom material selection in Design Space put more several material settings at your fingertips

5. Design Anytime. Anywhere.

Design on your computer, iPad, or iPhone with Design Space–free, cloud-based, easy-to-use software that lets you edit, customize, and preview projects. Choose from ready-to-make projects and thousands of Cricut images, or upload your designs. Download the Design Space app for iOS to craft on the go, and try our new offline feature to design without an Internet connection!

6. Your Designs. Our Tools. Endless Possibilities.

Are you a designer? Then this one's for you! Upload and cut out your artwork free. Upload files, and turn your masterpieces into home décor, cards, gifts, fashion, and more.

7. Go Wireless.

The Cricut Explore Air 2 offers wireless cutting, writing, and scoring with built-in Bluetooth.

8. Print Then Cut.

Print full-color images and patterns, then watch your Cricut Explore machine cut them out for you! There are more than 50,000 printable images and 920 printable patterns in Design Space. Or you can simply upload your own!

Cricut Explore Air 2 Blades

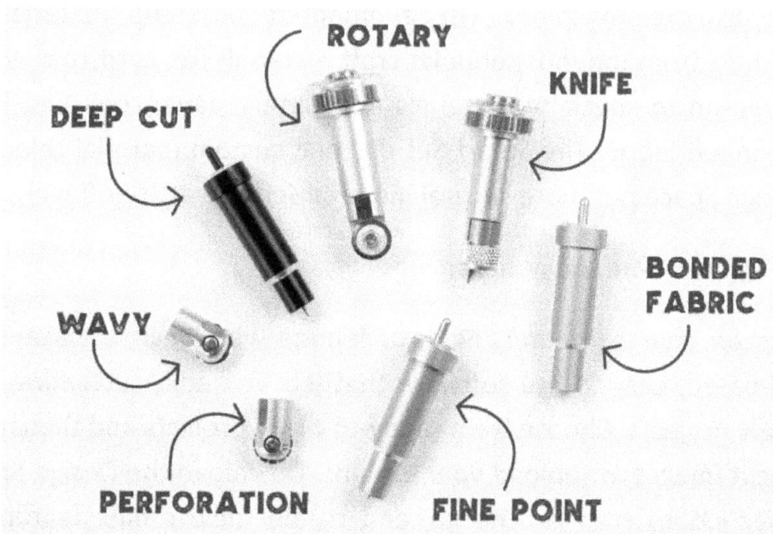

Fine Point Blade

The Fine Point Blade is designed to cut light and mid-weight materials like vinyl, iron-on, cardstock, and posterboard. The blade is made out of premium German carbide for longer-lasting cuts and sharpness. This is the blade I use for the majority of my projects when using the Cricut Explore Air 2.

Bonded Fabric Blade

Designed specifically to cut bonded fabrics the Fabric Blade is made of German carbide as well. It allows you to cut a variety of lightweight fabrics that have a backing on them. This is a great option for creating appliques!

Deep-Point Blade

Need to cut thick materials like stiff felt, leather, cardboard, or even magnet? This blade does the trick! The steep angle of the blade (60 degrees vs 45) allows you to cut thicker materials than the Fine Point Blade. With this blade, you can cut materials up to 1.5mm in thickness.

Scoring Stylus

The Scoring Stylus is a tool that allows you to created folds on your materials. It's perfect for making boxes and card making.

Foil Transfer Kit

The "Foil Transfer Kit" allows you to create beautiful and crisp foil effects on your projects. It's compatible with the Cricut Maker and any of the Explore family machines. This kit is 3 tools in 1; to best suit your project, Cricut comes with fine, medium, and bold tips.

Cricut Pens

The Cricut Pens are amazing, because not only you can cut and score, but you can also write on your materials. The Pens allow you to create a more personalized project.

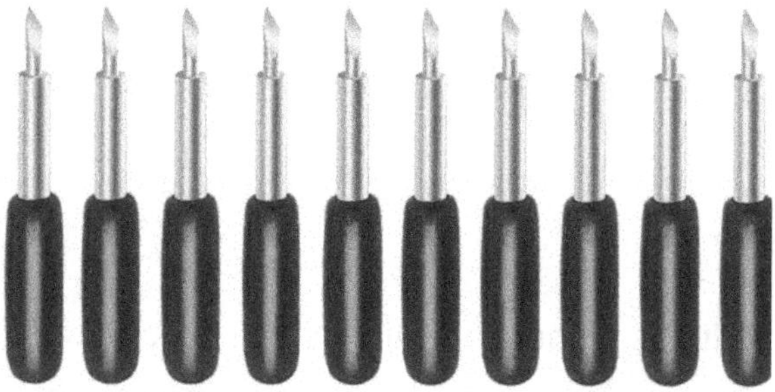

Print Then Cut

This is not the tool itself but is a feature that allows you to print – on white color paper – your designs and then cut them. This is great if you are into planner stickers, patterns, card making, etc.

Explore Air 2 Print And Cut

The Cricut Explore Air 2 offers the ability to print and cut images. Use your home printer to bring your images to life and cut them with perfect precision on the Cricut Explore Air 2. It's the ideal way to create beautiful gift tags, stickers, and cutouts.

Cartridge Adapter

There is an accessory adapter on the Explore Air 2 machine which is compatible with Cricut cartridges, so you still have access to all of your most loved images.

What Do The Cricut Maker And Explore Air 2 Have In Common?

The Cricut Maker and Explore Air 2 are both EXCELLENT machines. You can feel the quality; everything seems so sturdy and well made. I am quite impressed. You won't be disappointed. Every time I have ordered from Cricut everything is packed to perfection and you can just feel that they truly care for what they do.

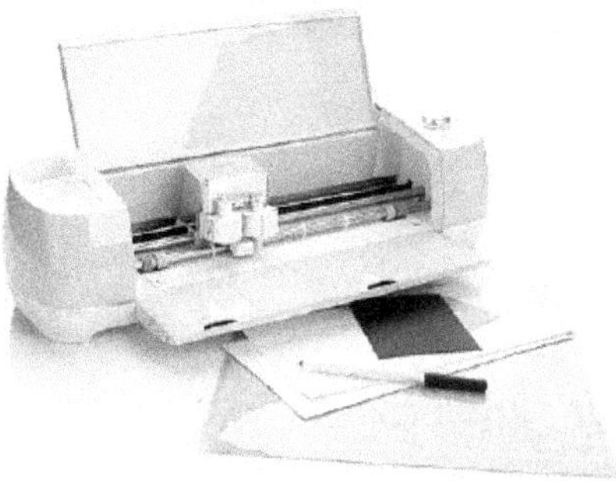

CRICUT EXPLORE AIR 2	CRICUT MAKER
Wireless Bluetooth Technology	Wireless Bluetooth Technology
Cut 100+ materials from vellum to leather	Cuts 100+ of materials from vellum to wood
Double Tool Holder	Double Tool Holder
Smart Dial for easy material settings	**Adaptive Tool System** with expandable suite of tools!
Cuts some fabrics with backing material	**Rotary Blade** to cut any fabric without backing
Deep-Cut Blade slices thick materials (ie, foam)	**Knife Blade** slices heavy materials (ie, basswood)
Use the **Scoring Stylus** to create score lines	**Scoring Wheels** to create extra-deep score lines
"Print Then Cut" on white paper	"Print Then Cut" on white, colored, <u>or</u> patterned paper
Plug in physical cartridges to upload to Design Space	Access to 100+ digital sewing patterns
Designed for Crafters	Designed for MAKERS

Cricut Explore Air 2 & Cricut Maker Side By Side

With both machines you will have:

- Both machines work with the same software Cricut Design Space for free
- Upload your personalized designs and projects
- FREE Ready to cut projects: Each machine comes with more than 50 free projects. Normally ready to cut projects cost money that you can get access by individual purchase or via a monthly or yearly subscription called Cricut Access
- They both can cut more than 100 materials – the MOST common ones – including paper, vinyl, fabric, leather, etc! To see the whole materials check out the full Cricut Guide.
- With both machines, you can Cut, Draw, Score and add foil effects with the "foil transfer kit."
- Both Machines come with a first Project for you to get familiar with your machine

How To Set Up Your Cricut Air Explorer 2 Machine

Completing the machine setup automatically registers the machine to your account. To set up your Cricut Explore, Explore One, Explore Air, Explore Air 2, or Cricut Maker machine, follow these steps:

Windows/Mac

- Plugin the machine and power it on.
- Connect the machine to your computer with the USB cord or pair it via Bluetooth.
- Go to design.cricut.com/setup in your browser.
- Download and install Design Space for Desktop (help article).

- Follow the on-screen instructions to sign in or create your Cricut ID, and set up your new machine.
- You will know the setup is complete when you are prompted to do a test cut.

IOS/Android

- Plugin the machine and power it on.
- Pair your Android or iOS device with a Cricut machine via Bluetooth.
- Download and install the Design Space app (help article).
- Launch the app, then sign in or create a Cricut ID.
- Tap the menu and select Machine Setup.
- Select your machine model and follow the on-screen prompts to complete the setup.
- You will know the setup is complete when you are prompted to do a test cut.

Tip: Your machine is automatically registered during machine setup. If you did not complete the setup when you connected your machine to your computer for the first time, re-connect your machine, go to design.cricut.com/setup or select New Machine Setup through the Design Space account menu, and follow the on-screen prompts.

How To Cut Heavyweight And Lightweight Materials

Which Cricut Machine Mat Should You Use?

Decisions, decisions, decisions! Are you wondering, "Which mat should I use for my Cricut projects?" Or perhaps pondering, "Which Cricut machine mat will work with this material?" We understand it can be a little bit overwhelming at first, so here's a little guidance for selecting the best mat for your Cricut Maker or Cricut Explore machine projects. If you have an older machine, see which mats are compatible with your machine.

There Are 4 Different Cricut Machine Mats:

- LightGrip Machine Mat
- StandardGrip Machine Mat
- StrongGrip Machine Mat
- FabricGrip Machine Mat

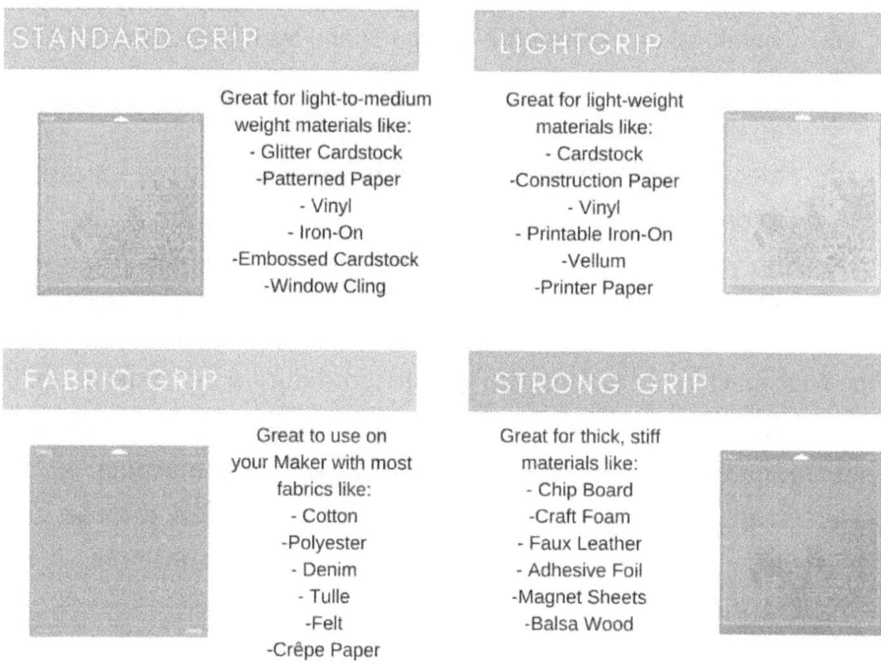

Each of these mats is used to cut different types of materials (from popular lightweight materials like copy paper and washi tape sheets to heavyweight materials like faux leather and corrugated cardboard). The material you are cutting with your machine can help determine which mat to use.

1. LightGrip Machine Mat

The blue LightGrip Machine Mat has just the right level of grip to hold your material firmly in place during cutting, yet it allows for easy removal of the lighter weight material when you are finished cutting. The LightGrip Machine Mat is perfect for lightweight materials, including:

- ❖ Printer paper
- ❖ Vellum
- ❖ Light cardstock paper
- ❖ Thin scrapbook paper
- ❖ Washi sheets
- ❖ Wrapping paper
- ❖ Construction paper

Party poppers are just one example of projects that the LightGrip Machine Mat can make using thin scrapbook paper. Try making this project for party poppers. Or, use washi sheets to create a monogram piece of wall art. If you're up for more of a challenge, try this paper flower boutonniere.

2. StandardGrip Machine Mat

The green StandardGrip Machine Mat may be the most widely used. It is perfect for a wide range of medium-weight materials, including:

- ❖ Cardstock
- ❖ Textured paper
- ❖ Embossed cardstock
- ❖ Iron-on (commonly known as HTV)
- ❖ Vinyl
- ❖ Pattern paper
- ❖ Infusible Ink transfer sheets

Try making a "Love You More" sign or blanket throw with iron-on using the StandardGrip Machine Mat. Or, here's an easy "Happy Birthday" box that uses cardstock.

3. StrongGrip Machine Mat

The purple StrongGrip Machine Mat offers a strong hold surface suitable and engineered for heavyweight materials. This mat is perfect for heavyweight materials, including:

- Thick cardstock
- Glitter cardstock
- Magnet material
- Chipboard
- Posterboard
- Matboard
- Fabric with stiffener
- Corrugated cardboard
- (Faux) leather and suede
- Wood

Use the StrongGrip Machine Mat to create easy photo magnets with printable magnet sheets. If you are an avid maker that likes to experiment with a multitude of materials, the StrongGrip mat complements the knife blade for Cricut Maker. It's a must-have combination for cutting through thick materials such as wood, matboard, chipboard, and craft foam. Create your own mat board picture frame with the StrongGrip mat and knife blade combo, then add textured accents using the debossing tip.

4. FabricGrip Machine Mat

The FabricGrip Machine Mat has a light adhesive machine mat that is made for a variety of fabrics. If you are a sewer, this is a must-have addition to your Cricut collection. It is specifically designed to secure fabrics for cutting, with easy release, and works as a complement to Rotary Blade or Bonded-Fabric Blade projects. The mat has is engineered with a stronger, denser material that withstands added pressure of those blades. And, don't forget, the Rotary Blade is included with your Cricut Maker machine!

This mat is perfect for all fabrics, including:

- Bonded fabrics for Cricut Explore machines
- Unbacked fabrics for Cricut Maker

Cricut Machine Mat Tips:

- Cricut machine mats have been optimized for a variety of popular crafting materials. Each machine mat has just the right grip to hold your material firmly in place during cutting, then easily remove it when finished.
- Don't neglect the clear film cover that comes with your mat! Return the clear film cover onto the mat when storing to keep it free from lint and dust.
- Utilize tools for removing your cuts from the mat: the spatula allows you to carefully remove your cut from the mat, whereas the scraper tool will help remove all the excess pieces quickly.
- Consider purchasing mats in various sizes. Cricut machine mats for Cricut Maker and Cricut Explore machines typically come in two different sizes: 12" x 12" and 12" x 24".
- Only use recommended materials with each corresponding mat for longer life and better performance.
- LightGrip or blue mat for lightweight materials
- StandardGrip or green mat for medium-weight materials

- StrongGrip or purple mat for heavyweight materials
- FabricGrip or pink mat for fabrics

Use a combination of the different mats to help you create mixed-media projects such as this chipboard cactus of coasters.

How To Design With Cricut Machine

Cricut Design Space Tips & Tricks You'll Want To Know

There is no doubt a steep learning curve to using a Cricut machine. And while the machine itself (not to mention all the materials it can cut!) is one thing, by far the most questions I get from readers are related to Cricut Design Space: Cricut's design software. Cricut Design Space itself is not difficult; but admittedly, some things are not as intuitive as many of us would like them to be. And when you are just getting started, it can sometimes feel like even the most basic techniques are overly complicated. However, once you get rolling on your first few projects, you will soon see that Cricut Design Space does include everything you need to create amazing projects AND that there are lots of great shortcuts that make creating not only easy but efficient! Today, I want to share 20 Cricut Design Space tips you may not know. These tricks and hacks come from spending HOURS in the program myself, and are sure to save you tons of time and stress so that you can create anything your heart desires with ultimate ease and confidence!

I'm going to break these Cricut Design Space Tips and Tricks into two categories:

1. On The Design Canvas: Where you create your projects and edit/manipulate your designs

2. On The Cut Screen: The series of screens that allow you to set your cut settings after you click the green "Make It" button

Cricut Design Space Tips – On The Design Canvas

1. Customize Your Designs With Weld, Contour, And Slice: Any image, whether it's one from the Design Space Image Library or one you upload yourself, can be endlessly changed, customized, and personalized using the three main editing tools: Weld, Contour, and Slice. All three of these tools are located along the bottom right-side toolbar and will only highlight when the functions are available for a specific design.

At first glance, these tools may not seem like they do much. Nonetheless, they are incredibly powerful and are the keys to completely personalizing your designs.

2. Experiment With Your Search Terms: I've learned that the search function in the Design Space Image Library can be a little particular. A pretty generic term that I think should yield all sorts of images sometimes won't. Yet if I change a single word or even a single letter, suddenly more images populate. As such, I recommend playing around with a lot of search terms to find exactly what you're looking for.

3. See More From The Same Cartridge: When you use the search function, you may find one image that you love amidst a whole variety of other images that you don't. What do you do when you want to see more images similar to the ones you like? The best place is to start is with the cartridge (set) that it came from. To quickly and easily access the cartridge, simply click the small information circle (i) in the bottom right-hand corner of each image within the Design Space Image Library (below left). It will open up the image details with a clickable (green) link that will take you to the full set of images (below right)! This is my favorite way to find coordinating/matching images to the one I found via search!

4. Utilize Free Images & Text: I am a HUGE fan of the Cricut Access memberships if you are a habitual crafter like I am. However, I realize that many people, especially newbies, may not want to spend money just to practice cutting on their machines, especially not at first. If you're just learning your way around, want to see your machine in action, and/or want to keep your crafting costs to a minimum, be sure to utilize the FREE resources within Cricut Design Space.

To find FREE images...use the Filter within the Design Space Image Library. Simply select the "Free" option to see an array of images you can insert into your projects at no cost!

To find FREE fonts...Your Cricut machine can cut any font you have installed on your computer. This not only means that you can cut any font that came pre-installed on your computer, but also any awesome font you find and download from some of your favorite free sites such as Font Squirrel or DaFont. To find the fonts you can use without incurring additional charges, simply choose "My Fonts" from the font menu filter. This will show you ALL the fonts installed on your computer, as well as any Cricut fonts you may have purchased (either individually or via a Cricut Access pass), and is a great way to ensure you are using fonts you won't have to pay for!

5. Re-Color Quickly: The Color Sync tool is a great way to save time on your projects and ensure you are using the same colors across different designs. When you place several designs onto your Design Canvas, you may end up with various shades of the same color (e.g., 3 different greens, 4 different blues, etc.) Instead of selecting each layer to re-color it, navigate to the Color Sync tool along with the right-hand tool panel. Here, you can not only see all the colors currently in use on your project, but you can also drag-and-drop any layer of your design to another color already represented. Whether you want to keep consistent colors across your designs or quickly make certain layers a particular color for more efficient cutting, this is the quickest and easiest way to do it!

6. The Hide Tool: When I am working on a project, I often pull lots and lots of images to play with. However, when it comes time to cut out my projects, I rarely need to cut everything on my canvas. Also, there are times when I just need to cut/re-cut one part of the design. Instead of deleting images off my canvas simply to avoid cutting them, I will "hide" them by clicking the eye symbol next to the exact image on the right-hand Layers Panel. Any image that is "hidden" is not removed from your canvas, but it will not be included when you send your project to be cut. The "Hide" symbol toggles on/off, making it oh-so-simple to cut only what you need and/or keep your design canvas clutter-free without losing track of images you may still want to play with!

7. Change Any Line To Cut, Score, Or Draw: Once upon a time, if you wanted a line to be drawn or scored (rather than cut), you had to find a design with those specific attributes. However, a recent change to Design Space now allows ANY line to be easily changed from cut to score to draw with the simple Linetype drop-down menu on the top toolbar:

Most designs will populate on your canvas as a "Cut" design. But you can easily change the outline of the image to be drawn (using the pens) or scored (using the scoring tool or scoring wheel). Just make sure your layers are un-grouped and un-attached to change how your design will ultimately be created.

8. Manipulate Patterns: You can now also change how the image is filled with the new Fill tool along the top toolbar. With an individual layer selected, you can swap out colors or assign a pattern to the inside of the image. Filling the images with one of the pre-loaded patterns is a fun way to add interest to your projects without relying on patterned scrapbook paper or cardstock. In addition to countless designs being available, you can also manipulate the scale and orientation of the pattern by clicking "Edit Pattern" in the Pattern menu (under Fill). NOTE: The pattern option can only be used via the Print-then-Cut technique.

9. Use Keyboard Shortcuts: There are buttons on the Design Space canvas for almost every command you can think of (e.g., Duplicate, Delete, Copy, Cut, Paste, etc.) These buttons exist on the corners of the images themselves, the top toolbar, and in the right-hand Layers Panel. However, to save time, try using many of the keyboard shortcuts that work in other computer programs. Specifically, these shortcuts come in quite handy and can save you a lot of time when working on big projects: Copy (control C) | Paste (control V) | Delete (delete button) | Undo (control Z).

10. Use Slice To Crop: One tool that may appear to be missing from Cricut Design Space is a Crop tool. Yes, admittedly, I've often yearned for a tool that would allow me to quickly and easily slice designs apart or shave off certain details as you can in many other programs. However, there is a workaround! You can use the Slice Tool in conjunction with the free shapes (e.g., circle, square) to achieve what a typical Crop tool would do. It can be a little tedious and not at all intuitive, so check out my full tutorial on how to do it here.

Cricut Design Space Tips – On The Cut Screen

Once you finish designing your project and send the images to be cut via the green "Make It" button, you might think your ability to manipulate the project is through. However, there are LOTS of things you can do on the cut screen itself to not only save time but also save on materials. These 10 Cricut Design Space Tips are some of the best things to know about Cricut Design Space, so let's run through them!

11. Move Items Around On The Mat: Did you know you can move the items around the mat on the cut screen itself? While the Design Space software will auto-populate your images onto the mats based on their color and orientation, it may not be exactly where you want them to be.

Simply by dragging and dropping the images, you can move a cut anywhere on the mat and even rotate it using the handles on the upper right-hand corner. This not only allows you to scrunch things up tighter than the software originally suggests, but it also ensures your cut is precisely where you need it to be (like if you are trying to use a scrap or oddly-shaped piece of material). Just make sure you match the grid lines on the screen to the grid lines on your mat to ensure your design fits your material wherever you have it!

12. Move Images From One Mat To Another: In addition to moving images around a single mat, you can also move any image from one mat to another (without having to go back to the design canvas and change its color). Simply click on the 3 dots on the upper left-hand corner of any image on your cut mat. Then select "Move to another mat"...Design Space will then allow you to choose which mat you'd like to place that specific image on...

13. Save Your Most Commonly Used Cut Materials: I just discovered this feature and I'm somewhat embarrassed that it took me so long. When I was using my Cricut Explore Air 2, I wouldn't utilize the Custom materials option very often because I mostly had my machine set to Vinyl, Cardstock, Iron-On, etc. But when I transitioned to the Maker, I learned I had to use the Custom Materials menu within Cricut Design Space every time because there is no dial to select the material you are cutting.

14. Skip And Repeat Mats: One of the nicest things about how Design Space works is that you don't have to pay much attention once you send your design to cut. As long as you feed the right color and size paper into your machine just as it's shown on the left side of your cut screen, your project should turn out as you designed it! However, you may find that you want to skip around which mat is cut next, re-cut a particular mat, or skip a mat altogether. Thankfully, it's super easy and doesn't require exiting out of the cut screen. Before you load your mat into the machine, you can manually select which mat will be cut next simply by selecting/clicking it on the left-hand side. The machine will automatically jump to whatever mat you manually select…

15. Connect Several Machines At Once: I realize most people likely do not have more than one Cricut machine. But if you do, you CAN connect both machines to your Design Space account at the same time either via Bluetooth or USB. And don't worry about cutting the wrong design out with the wrong machine. No matter how many machines you have connected (1 or several), your very first step on the final cut screen is to select which machine you want to use via the top dropdown menu. In this way, you can always be sure you're using the intended machine for your project!

16. Edit Cut Settings For ANY Material: One question I get a lot is related to cutting specific materials. For example, even with the machine set to Vinyl, some folks have told me that their Cricut won't sufficiently cut through it. Thankfully, you can adjust the settings for ANY material (including depth, blade, and how many passes the machine will make) right from the Materials menu.

Here's How You Do It:

- On the Cut Screen, you will have the option to select "Materials" (if you're not on a Maker, set your Explore machine dial to Custom)
- Then select Browse All Materials (small green letters on top of the menu)
- Down at the bottom, in small green letters, it says Material Settings
- From there, you can select any material and adjust the settings...to include how many passes the machine should make and the depth of each pass!
- If you find that for some reason your machine won't sufficiently cut through a material you use all the time, this is a great way to adjust the settings so you don't have to make manual adjustments every single time!

17. Easily Adjust Cut Pressure: While it is awesome to be able to adjust the settings of any material, sometimes you just need a little more or a little less pressure for your material to be cleanly cut through. To do so... after you select your material on the final cut screen, alter the pressure to be either Default, More, or Less via the dropdown menu:

- This is a great way to quickly and easily get your cutting depth right without having to fuss with the custom settings!

18. Fill Mat By Changing Project Copies: I will admit that one of my favorite features from the old Cricut machines isn't available anymore: the Autofill feature. I loved that I could put a single star on my design canvas, select my paper size, and then select "Autofill." The machine would then fill up my paper with as many stars as could comfortably fit. While this exact feature is missing from Design Space, there is a pretty easy workaround.

On the very first cut screen, there is an option at the very top to set your "Project Copies." This function allows you to cut whatever is on your design canvas as many times as you want. Although it may take some trial-and-error to figure out how many copies you need to fill up the mat, it's a much quicker solution than playing around with duplicates on the design canvas itself.

19. Set Mirror On The Cut Screen: There will be times, especially when you are working with Iron-On projects, that you will need to cut your design in reverse (aka: Mirror). Although you can horizontally flip your design on the design canvas, there is an option to Mirror your designs on the cut screen itself:

This not only enables you to mirror just the mats/images you need to be flipped around but also allows you to create and tweak your design un-flipped on the design screen (which is much easier to look at and customize).

20. Fool-Proof Instructions: One of the best things about taking the time to select your custom material on the cut screen is that Design Space will provide you with invaluable reminders to ensure your projects turn out just right. For example, when you select "Iron-On," you will be given the reminders to Mirror your designs and place the shiny side of your vinyl down onto the mat. When you select something like Chipboard, it will prompt you to check your blade, secure your material to the mat, etc. The key here is not to overlook these subtle instructions because they really can save you lots of valuable time and product!

Keyboard Shortcuts

Function	Windows	Mac
Select All	Ctrl A	CMD A
Group	Ctrl G	CMD G
Ungroup	Ctrl U	CMD U
Copy to clipboard	Ctrl C	CMD C
Paste from clipboard	Ctrl V	CMD V
Cut to clipboard	Ctrl X	CMD X
Print/Cut/Go		CMD P
Quit/Exit CCR	Ctrl E	CMD Q
Open & Close Menus and keypad drawer	Tab	Tab
Undo	Ctrl Z	CMD Z
Redo	Ctrl + Shift Z	CMD +Shift Z or CMD Y
New project	Ctrl N	CMD N

Open project	Ctrl O	CMD O
Save	Ctrl S	CMD S
Save As	Ctrl + Shift S	
Quick Type/Add Text Box	Ctrl T	CMD T
Send Front		open [
Send Back		close]
Send Forward	] or Ctrl up arrow	CMD Up arrow
Send Backward	[or Ctrl down arrow	CMD Down arrow
Exit Hide Contours and Edit Group modes	Esc	Esc
Nudge objects	Right/Left/Up/Down arrows	Right/Left/Up/Down arrows
Big Nudge objects	Shift Right/Left/Up/Down arrows	SHFT Right/Left/Up/Down arrows
Delete selected objects	Del	Del
Zoom in	Z + click on mat	Z + click on mat
Zoom out	Z + Alt + click on mat	Z + Alt + click on mat
Scale non proportionally by	Alt + Click on height or width handle	CMD mouse down

height or width		
Pan screen (mouse cursor changes to a hand)	Space bar and drag screen up or down	Space bar and drag screen up or down

Using Fonts In Design Space

Design Space makes it easy to personalize your project using text and different fonts. You can use Cricut fonts as well as any system font installed on your computer, iOS device, or Android device.

Adding Text

Insert text onto the Canvas by selecting the Text tool from the panel on the left side of the Canvas. On the iOS or Android App, select Text at the bottom-left of the screen.

Windows/Mac: The Text Edit bar and a text box will appear.

iOS/Android: The font list will open.

Select the font you wish to use. Then type your text in the text box. Use the "Return" key after a line of text if you want to create a new line of text in the same text box. On a Windows/Mac computer, you can type your text before selecting a font. The text will render on the Canvas in a default font.

Select an area outside the text box to close it. Now you can move, size, and rotate the text.

To edit your text, simply double-click or double-tap on the text. The text box will open. Options to change the font, font style, font size, letter spacing, line spacing, etc. are accessed through the Edit bar at the top of the Canvas (Windows/Mac) or Edit tool at the bottom of the Canvas (iOS/Android) when your text is selected.

Tools You Need To Know To Edit Text In Cricut Design Space

- **Font:** Choose the fonts you would like to use. You can filter by Cricut fonts or System fonts (these are the fonts on your computer).
- **Style:** Choose a font style, like bold, italic, etc. This only works if the font you have installed already has different styles.
- **Font Size:** Pretty self-explanatory, but you can use the drop-down, arrows, or manually type in a number to change the size of the font.
- **Letter Space:** Change the spacing between each letter. The higher the number, the further apart the letters. It's okay to use negative numbers.
- **Line Space:** Change the spacing between paragraphs.
- **Alignment:** Align the text to the left, right, or center.
- **Advanced:** This will ungroup certain aspects of a font. If it's one line, it will ungroup letters, so you can move them individually. If it's two or more, you can ungroup by line.
- **Weld:** Combines shapes and letters to create one cut line. Learn more about the Weld Tool.

How To Edit Text In Cricut Design Space

- First, you'll create a new document from your dashboard, then click on the type tool.
- Type in the box, then choose your font. If you ever need to edit your text, just double-click on the word and the type cursor will appear.

- At this point, I like to change the size and alignment. You can change the size on the toolbar, or you can simply drag the word by the bottom icon (the one that looks like two arrows).
- You've probably noticed the spacing is pretty far apart. To move them closer together, use the Letter Spacing Tool. Use the down arrow to move it closer, or enter in a negative number manually.
- The fonts will still be a little wonky, so go to ADVANCED and click on UNGROUP TO LETTERS. Now, you can move each letter closer together so each letter is connecting. I like doing this with script bounce letter fonts because it doesn't have to be placed perfectly.
- Now, you'll select all the letters and click on WELD.
- Now, you're ready to cut or create the rest of your design!

Selecting A Font

The Text Edit tool in Cricut Design Space works very similarly to the Image Edit tool when sizing, rotating, and positioning text. It also makes finding the right font and editing text simple so you can easily personalize your projects. The bounding box is the box that appears around your text when it is selected. Round "handles" in each corner of the bounding box allow you to make a quick edit.

Writing With Fonts

You can use Cricut pens with your Cricut machine to write any font by changing the line type of your text to "Write" instead of "Cut". However, Design Space offers several Cricut fonts specifically designed to be drawn with a pen and not cut. While most fonts will trace the outside of the letters, "writing style" fonts feature letters with single strokes, so they are the most similar to handwritten text. When selecting a font, you can choose a font with a Writing style.

Using System Fonts

System fonts are fonts that are installed on your computer or mobile device. Design Space automatically accesses your system fonts each time you sign in and allows you to use them in Design Space projects for free. When downloading fonts to your computer or device, follow the instructions on the font size or app to ensure that the font is successfully installed on your computer or device. Because system fonts are installed on a particular device, the available system fonts may vary between devices.

How To Install Fonts On A Windows PC/ Mac

Select your platform from below for step-by-step instructions:

- Windows/Mac
- iOS/ Android

Windows/Mac

- Select "Text" from the design panel to the left of the canvas.
- The Text Edit bar will appear. You can either type your text first or select a font first.
- Click on the Font drop-down menu. Then select the "System" index. The font list will refresh and display only the fonts installed on that computer.
- Select the desired font. If you have already typed some text on your design screen it will change to reflect your selection. If you have not yet typed text, the text that you proceed to add will appear on the canvas in the selected font.

iOS

- Select "Text" at the bottom of the Canvas screen.

- The font list will appear.
- Select the "System" index. The font list will refresh and display only the fonts installed on that device.
- Select the desired font, then type your text. It will render on the Canvas in the selected font.

Android

- Select "Text" at the bottom of the screen.
- You will be prompted to select your font from a font list that will display all available fonts including those installed on that mobile device. System fonts will be labeled "System".
- Scroll or search the list to find a system font to select.
- Select the desired font, then type your text. It will appear on the Canvas in the selected font.

Note: Because system fonts are not designed by Cricut, some may have design components that are not compatible with Design Space. This may result in a failure to import into Design Space, or unusual behavior when used in Design Space.

How To Use Images In Cricut Design Space

Image How to Upload Images on Cricut Design Space On

- Windows/Mac
- On iOS device:
- On Android device:

Uploading Images into Design Space

Design Space gives you the ability to upload your images for free and converts them into cuttable shapes. There are two different types of uploaded images: **Basic And Vector.**

- Basic Images, also known as raster images, include .jpg, .bmp, .png, and .gif file types. These files are uploaded as a single layer, and you can edit the image during the upload process. These are also known as raster images.
- Vector Images include .svg and .dxf file types. These files are uploaded as previously designed and will automatically be separated into layers after uploading and saving.

Select a platform from below to view step-by-step instructions to upload basic and vector images.

Note: DXF files are not supported in Design Space for iOS and Android at this time.

Windows/Mac

Step 1 - To begin an image upload, select Upload on the design panel to the left of the Canvas. A window will open which prompts you to choose image or pattern upload. Upload Image allows you to work with basic image types, including .jpg, .bmp, .png, and .gif image files as well as vector images, including .svg and .dxf files. To begin, select Upload Image.

Step 2 - Select Browse to open the file selector and locate the image you want to use from your computer, or simply drag and drop the file into the upload window. If you select .jpg, .gif, .png, or .bmp file to upload, you will be taken through the Basic image upload flow. If you select a .svg or .dxf, you will be taken through the Vector image upload flow.

Option 1 – Basic Image Upload:

Select the .jpg, .gif, .png, or .bmp file you want to upload. Then select Open in the file selector or drag and drop the file into the Design Space image upload window. Decide if your image is simple, moderately complex, or complex based on the descriptions found on the screen. Click "Continue."

In this step, you'll define the cut lines of your image. Use the Select & Erase, Erase, and Crop tools to remove the unwanted background from your image. The checkerboard background indicates the areas that have been removed and will not cut. The solid areas represent the image you will use on the design screen.

Once you have removed the unwanted areas, select Preview to show the cut lines of your image. If the image doesn't appear as desired, select Hide preview to return to the editing view and continue removing portions of the image until you are satisfied with the preview. Once the image looks how you want it, select Continue.

Name your image and tag it (if desired) for easy searching later. Decide if you want to save your image as a Print Then Cut or as a Cut image. Saving as a Print Then Cut image will preserve the entire image, including internal colors and patterns, and add it to the design screen as a Print Then Cut image. Saving as a Cut image will save only the outer silhouette as the image cut path.

When you are done, select Save. You will return to the Upload screen. The new image will appear in the Uploaded Images Library at the bottom of the screen. To add the image to your project, click on the image to select it, then click Insert Images to add it to your design screen.

Option 2 – Vector Image Upload:

Select the .svg or .dxf file you want to upload. Then select Open in the file selector, or drag and drop the file into the Design Space image upload window. Tip: Design Space can work with files created from other design software. The files can include solid colors or solid color fills, outlined text, or layers. However, if you use a layered image, you should ensure that in the original file the layers are ungrouped.

Name your image and tag it (if desired) for easier searching later. Then select Save.

You will return to the Upload screen. The new image will appear in the Uploaded Images Library at the bottom of the screen. To add the image to your design screen, click on the image to select it, then select Insert Images to add it to your design screen.

Vector images will appear on your canvas as a grouped image. If ungrouped, the image layers can be moved and sized separately.

Tip: Your uploaded images also are available on the Images screen. You can search by image name or tag, or you can select Uploaded from the filter in the upper right of the Images screen.

Important: All images shown are for illustration purposes only. Cricut encourages you to respect the intellectual property rights of others and only make copies of images you own and are authorized to use.

On Ios Device:

To begin an image upload, tap the Upload tool on the bottom toolbar.

Choose to take a photo, select from the Camera Roll, browse files, or open your uploaded images.

If you choose "Browse files," you will be able to select any file storage applications available on your device (i.e. iCloud, Dropbox, Google Drive). Select the location where you have stored your image file to continue browsing and locate your image. This may look different depending on which version of iOS is running on your device.

If the image you upload is a vector image (SVG), the cut paths for the image are already defined, and it is ready to be saved to your uploaded images library. Enter a name for the image and select "Save" in the upper right corner of the screen.

Tip: When the image has been saved, your Uploaded Images library will open. Select an image to insert onto the canvas and work on your project. Pull down to refresh your uploaded images as needed.

If the image is basic (JPG, PNG, BMP, GIF), which it would be if you take a photo or select an image from the Camera Roll, the next step is to clean up the image. Cleaning up the image removes areas of the image you don't want, and defines the cut lines of the image. There are three clean up tools:

Remove: quickly removes connected areas of the same color. Tap on an area, or tap and hold to select a precise area. Pinch to zoom in for more precise edits. Use the slider to increase or decrease the strength of the tool. The checkered background indicates areas that have been removed and will not cut.

A cut preview will appear in the upper right of your image as you clean up the image, and it will change to reflect your edits. Tap on the preview to enlarge it; flick to minimize it.

Erase: Erase areas of the image. Drag one finger across areas of the image you want to remove. Adjust the slider to increase or decrease the size of the eraser. Pinch outward to zoom in for more precise edits.

Crop: Focuses your work area by trimming the edges of your image. Tap and drag the handles in the corners to set the crop area, then tap Done to crop the image, or tap the circular arrow in the center bottom of the screen to reset the image.

When you are done cleaning up the image, tap Next in the upper right corner of the screen.

The Refine screen is next. Here you can make a few final adjustments to the image before saving it to your library. Tap the image preview in the upper right to toggle between the print view and the cut view.

Despeckle: Quickly eliminates small artifacts. Drag the slider further to the right to remove larger artifacts.

Smooth: Simplifies jagged lines. Simply tap Smooth as many times as needed. Tap Reset to start over.

When you are finished refining the image, tap Next in the upper right corner.

Name your image, choose whether to save it as a Cut Image or as a Print then Cut image. Then click Save in the upper right corner of the screen.

When the image has been saved, your Uploaded Images library will open. Select an image to insert onto the canvas and work on your project. Pull down to refresh your uploaded images as needed.

On Android Device:

To begin an image upload, tap the Upload tool on the bottom toolbar.

Choose to take a photo, select from the photo library, or open your uploaded images.

If you choose "Select from Photo Library", you will be able to select any file storage applications available on your device (i.e., Google Drive, Onedrive, Dropbox, etc). Select the location where you have stored your image file to continue browsing and locate your image. This may look different depending on which version of Android is running on your device.

If the image you upload is a vector image (SVG), the cut paths for the image are already defined, and it is ready to be saved to your uploaded images library. Enter a name for the image and select "Save" in the upper right corner of the screen.

Tip: When the image has been saved, your Uploaded Images library will open. Select an image to insert onto the canvas and work on your project.

If the image is basic (JPG, PNG, BMP, GIF), which it would be if you take a photo or select an image from the Camera Roll, the next step is to clean up the image. Cleaning up the image removes areas of the image you don't want, and defines the cut lines of the image. There are three clean up tools:

Remove: Quickly removes connected areas of the same color. Tap on an area, or tap and hold to select a precise area. Pinch to zoom in for more precise edits. Use the slider to increase or decrease the strength of the tool. The checkered background indicates areas that have been removed and will not cut. A cut preview will appear in the upper right of your image as you clean up the image, and it will change to reflect your edits. Tap on the preview to enlarge it; flick to minimize it.

Erase: Erase areas of the image. Drag one finger across areas of the image you want to remove. Adjust the slider to increase or decrease the size of the eraser. Pinch outward to zoom in for more precise edits.

Crop: Focuses your work area by trimming the edges of your image. Tap and drag the handles in the corners to set the crop area, then tap Done to crop the image, or tap the circular arrow in the center bottom of the screen to reset the image.

When you are done cleaning up the image, tap Next in the upper right corner of the screen.

Name your image, choose whether to save it as a Cut Image or as a Print then Cut image. Then click Save in the upper right corner of the screen.

When the image has been saved, your Uploaded Images library will open. Select an image to insert onto the canvas and work on your project. Pull down to refresh your uploaded images as needed.

How To Clean A Cricut Machine

Cricut Cutting Problems: Tips For Cleaner Cuts

1. Use A Sticky Mat

Your Cricut mat needs to be pretty sticky to get clean cuts. So if your cuts aren't clean, the first thing you should do is change your mat. I usually switch to a new or newer mat and it solves my problem right away. If you can't afford a new mat, you can try washing your mat with dishwashing soap and allowing it to air dry to get it stickier, but I'll be honest — it might still not be sticky enough. A sticky mat can make all the difference. And I prefer the green mats over the blue mats.

2. Use A Clean, Sharp Blade

You need to make sure your Cricut blade is clean and sharp. I do this by taking a sheet of aluminum foil and balling it up like this. Then I remove the blade from its housing, depress the plunger, and stick it in and out of the aluminum ball CAREFULLY over and over maybe 50 times. This cleans any debris from the blade, like bits of paper or vinyl that might be stuck to the blade, and also seems to sharpen it. (It may not be sharpening it, but it works!) This technique works for the Fine-Point and Deep-Point Blades. This technique works GREAT for me and I haven't had to buy a new blade in over a year. I always do this to my blades when I'm about to cut something with really intricate cuts.

3. Use Quality Materials

Your material can make a big difference in how it cuts, too. For example, not all paper is created equal. If the fibers are weaker or shorter in the paper, which you usually find in lower quality paper, you'll get more tearing. So if your paper doesn't seem to be cutting well even after using a sticky mat and a clean blade, the paper itself could be the culprit. There have been many times when I've had an issue and then changed to a new paper only to have everything work perfectly. Cricut paper is high quality, so is Recollections.

4. Check Your Settings

You must have got the right settings for your material. I find it works best to indicate the material settings in Cricut Design Space rather than on your Cricut dial. To do this on a Cricut Explore, just rotate the dial to Custom and you'll be prompted to choose your material before you cut it. (Note that the Maker has no dial you are on "customer settings" by default.) And if that still doesn't seem to help, try increasing the pressure of your cut. This is why I almost always have "More" pressure on my cuts, it seems to always help me get those clean cuts.

5. Check Your Pattern

Not all patterns are going to cut cleanly. The smaller and more detailed and intricate they are, the harder it's going to be to cut them. Sometimes, they are just too small. So you can try making them larger if that is an option.

If that doesn't work or is not an option, you can try setting your material to Intricate Cuts if you're cutting cardstock. Or try the washi tape set if you're cutting vinyl. Neither of these is guaranteed to work, but it's worth a try. In the end, some patterns may just be too tiny or detailed to be cut without issues. This doesn't mean all is lost, however you may still be able to cut it and just clean it up with scissors or a knife later.

These are all the tips I use each time I go to cut something, and I nearly always have clean cuts on all three of my Cricuts because of it. It does require a certain mindset you have to go into a project knowing you might need to tinker with it a bit to get it to cut properly. Testing can help a LOT. The key is not to give up. Be persistent and try new things. It always works for me!

Cleaning The Cricut Machines

- Gently wipe exterior panels with a damp cloth.
- Immediately dry any excess moisture with a chamois or other soft cloth.

- Do not use chemicals or alcohol-based cleaners (including, but not limited to, acetone, benzene, and carbon tetrachloride) on the machine. Scratchy cleansers and cleaning tools should also be avoided. Do not dip the machine or any component of it in water.
- Keep away from food and liquids, try not to eat and drink while using the machine.
- Keep in a dry, dust-free location.
- Avoid excessive heat or cold, do not leave the machine in the car, where excessive heat may melt or damage plastic components.
- Do not expose to direct sunlight for an extended period

FabricGrip Mat: Tips And tricks

The FabricGrip mat is made of a stronger, denser material to withstand the intense cutting pressures associated with using the Rotary Blade, making it possible for your Cricut Maker to cut fabric without a fabric stabilizer!

Step 1 - Preparing Your Fabric

Cutting Fabric Down To Size

Before placing the fabric on your mat, be sure to cut it down to a size that will fit on the mat, but does not extend outside of the adhesive area. 12 x 12 and 12 x 24 are the standard sizes for the adhesive area on the FabricGrip mat. Fabric that extends outside of the adhesive area may pass under the wide rubber rollers on either side of the roller bar, which will grip the fabric, pulling it askew or causing it to get caught in the machine.

Ironing

If your fabric is fairly wrinkled, it is a good idea to iron it to remove any stubborn wrinkles. Bumps or bubbles in the fabric may result in imprecise cuts. The fabric should lay very flat on the mat.

Step 2 - Placing Your Fabric On The Mat

Grain

All fabrics have what is called a grain. This refers to the direction of the woven threads, which run parallel to the selvage edge of the fabric. Design Space helps you know how to place your fabrics on the mat so that the grain is going in the right direction. On the mat preview, if the number on the piece is upright, place the fabric on your mat so that the grain runs up and down on the mat. If the numbers are on their side, place the fabric on your mat so that the grain runs right and left on the mat.

Pretty Side Down

Place your fabric on the mat so that the printed or "pretty" side of the fabric is down on the mat. This way, it will be much easier to see the fabric pen markings that will later help you to assemble your pieces. If your fabric doesn't have a printed side, just place the "right" side, meaning the side of the fabric that will show when your item is finished, down on the mat.

Getting It To Stick

Lightly position your fabric over the adhesive area of the mat, then smooth it into the adhesive with your hands. If your fabric mat has some threads on it from previous projects, or if you notice that it isn't sticking well, use a brayer, or kitchen rolling pin, or even the cardboard roll from some paper towels, to securely adhere the fabric to the mat.

Final Checks And Cautions

If you can see that your fabric extends outside of the adhesive square, simply use a ruler and a hand-held rotary cutter to trim it. Watch out for stretchy fabrics! Do not stretch your fabric as you stick it to the mat. It will wrinkle and may also retract during cutting, both of which may ruin your cut results. If you notice that your fabric is stretched or wrinkled, simply pull the fabric up and reposition it.

Step 3 - Choosing The Right Blade

Design Space will tell you which blade to use based on the material setting you choose, but the FabricGrip mat was designed for use with the Rotary Blade. The FabricGrip mat can also be used with the Bonded-Fabric blade.

Step 4 - Removing The Fabric After Cutting

Once the cutting is done, we recommend removing the excess fabric first.

Avoid touching the adhesive when removing your cuts; oils from hands can make the adhesive less sticky. The Broad Tip Tweezers are a great tool for removing your cuts from the mat. For fabrics that have a loose weave or fray easily, use the spatula to remove the cuts from the mat. They may bunch up as you remove them, but a quick pass with the iron will straighten them out.

How To Clean Your Fabricgrip Cricut Mat

Earlier this year, when I was able to go to the Cricut Mountain Make-a-thon, Cricut introduced the new Cricut Maker machine along with the fabric mat to go with it. I was so excited about this FabricGrip Mat! After I got my machine, the very first thing that I cut was felt.

Well, that felt left a big mess on my mat that I wasn't too excited about. One of the things we were told at the Mountain

Make-a-thon was that you didn't need to worry about fabric strings and fibers being left on the mat, it would still hold, and it did. But, the OCD in me and my wanting to have a clean mat got the better of me, so I thought I'd clean it and today, I'm sharing with you How to Clean Your FabricGrip Cricut Mat. You won't believe how easy it is!

Once your FabricGrip Cricut Mat has lots of fibers and fabric strings on it, it may not hold the fabric as well as it originally did. Without really thinking about it, I would want to grab a wet wipe and scrub the mat off. That's what I do with my other Cricut mats, but that is NOT what you want to do with the FabricGrip mat. You can also use this trick with all of the mats if you prefer.

Get yourself some of the Cricut StrongGrip Transfer Tape and cut a piece the size of your mat. Stick it down on your mat and use a scraper to smooth it out and get it on there really well.

Then pull the transfer tape off. This is a picture of the transfer tape after. It got so much stuff off!

Now my mat is much cleaner and ready to be used for a while longer!

How To Clean Your Cricut Pink Mat

With the release of the Cricut Maker, Cricut also gave us a new cutting mat the pink FabricGrip mat. The Cricut Maker is purpose-built for cutting fabric (among hundreds of other materials) and the fabric mat is essential for getting perfect fabric cuts.

But how do you keep your mat clean? People are already finding it harder to keep their pink mats clean, so I wanted to write a post about everything I've learned about my mat. First, I want you to throw out everything you know about cleaning Cricut mats. This mat is different. After using my pink mats and chatting with my friends who are using them as well, we've realized they're more finicky than the other three mats.

1. **Don't Use Your Scraper**

First and foremost, put down the scraper! The adhesive on the pink mat is different than the other three mats and you can scrape it right off the mat. Read ahead for what you should do instead.

2. **Keep Your Hands Off**

The adhesive on the Cricut pink mat is more delicate than on the other mats. The oils in your fingers quickly break down the adhesive in the mat, causing it to lose its stick. Just be cautious with your mat and try to avoid touching the adhesive if possible. You can use a brayer to help adhere your fabric to your mat if that helps (don't press hard, just enough to adhere the fabric to the mat). Use tweezers to pick up your pieces off the mat so that you keep your fingers away from the adhesive. Don't try and pick loose threads off the mat either if you really must pick, use the tweezers.

3. **Threats Don't Matter**

Speaking of threads, if you're cutting fabric you'll notice that you end up with a lot of threads on your mat. Leave them. We're conditioned to having super clean mats because any little bump when cutting paper or vinyl can be detrimental to a project. The rotary blade, however, is its beast. It cuts right through loose threads if you put the fabric over it — they won't ruin your cuts at all.

4. **Transfer Tape**

If the threads are bugging you or are noticing they are affecting your cuts, then you can use a piece of transfer tape to pull up the loose threads and other debris. Just put it sticky side down and peel it up. People have found this to be hit or miss, so use this tip with caution and as a last resort.

5. **Tips For Felt**

If you're cutting felt on your Cricut Maker (which you want to do it cuts it beautifully), you have a couple of options that will help keep you from destroying your pink mat with fuzz.

First, you don't have to use your pink mat. I have been using older green mats that still have some stick to cut felt and that works just fine. Yes, the fibers stick but I'd rather gunk up my old mats than gunk up my pink mat. I'm saving that for fabric.

You can also back your felt in transfer tape and stick that to the mat. I haven't done this myself, but people have been having good luck with this. Just peel it off after the cut! The downside to this is that you're using transfer tape for every cut could get expensive depending on what you're cutting!

6. **Pushing The Mat Past Its Limits**

The Cricut pink mat has limits. If you are trying to do a lot of intricate cutting with the rotary blade, you may notice that the mat starts peeling. The rotary blade isn't meant to cut a circle smaller than 3/4". If you cut smaller circles than that, I believe you're putting even more pressure on the blade and mat and it's not designed to handle that kind of pressure and you'll start to see your mat peel.

7. Do Not Re-Stick Your Mat

There are a ton of tutorials out there to re-stick your Cricut mats. These tutorials involve water, baby wipes, GooGone, spray adhesive, painter's tape, prayers, tears of unicorns, and any other number of things. Like I said above, the pink mat's adhesive is different than the adhesive on the other mats and you will ruin your mat. The adhesive on the pink mat is designed to hold the fabric but release it easily. If I ever discover a way to re-stick this mat, I'll come back here and update this post! It's better to take care of your mat using the above tips rather than try and restore a destroyed mat.

How To Clean Your Cricut Cutting Mat (And Restick It After)

This article will cover how to clean and maintain your cutting mats whether you're using a Cricut mat or a Silhouette. We all know how frustrating it can be when you start a project, and your material won't stick to the surface of your cutting mat. The questions I get the most are about cleaning and resticking cutting mats, especially after they've been used to cut felt. I'll explain how you can get rid of all the built-up gunk. We'll go over resticking your cutting mat when it's no longer working and end with some tips and answers to your frequently asked questions.

How To Clean Your Mat (Method 1: Gentle Cycle)

When you find that your Cricut mat is no longer sticky enough to properly hold your materials, try these methods to clean your mat and breathe some life back into it. As your mat accumulates grime and debris with your loving use, move down the list to more potent cleaning methods. Be gentle with your mats, and they may even last you through multiple rounds of holiday parties.

1. **Sticky Lint Roller**

Run a sticky lint roller (or loop of masking tape) across your Cricut mat to remove dust, fibers, bits of paper, and hairs. This can be done every day, between projects, when you forget to cover your Cricut mats overnight, or simply whenever you notice bits and fibers accumulating on your mat. It's a great way to remove any remaining slivers or bits of paper, instead of trying to go after them all with tweezers. When the lint roller or masking tape is stickier than the mat, it pulls all the offending hairs and bits of paper right off the mat! It works especially well on the less-tacky cutting mats.

2. **Baby Wipes**

Gently wipe down with unscented, alcohol-free, bleach-free baby wipes. Lotion-free, cornstarch-free. You want the absolute plainest wipes you can find, so you aren't coating your cutting mats with additional lotions, oils, or solvents that could interfere with the stickiness or break down the adhesive.

- Let dry before using.
- Soap and warm water
- Wash with soap and warm water.
- Dish soap is the best to use, and again you want to use soap that is free of lotions that could gunk up your mat.
- Gently scrub with a cloth, soft brush, soft sponge, or magic eraser, and rinse well.
- Let dry completely before using.

The Results

Often enough, simply washing your mat will be enough to rejuvenate its original sticky glory! After your cutting mat has completely dried, test out its stickiness with a scrap of the material you'll be using for your next project or a clean finger. If your mat has weathered enough seasons of projects, or been washed and scrubbed one too many times, you'll need to turn to something a bit stronger.

How To Clean Your Mat (Method 2: Heavy Duty)

If those gentle cleaning methods don't restore your cutting mat's functionality, you can try breaking out the big guns and use an adhesive remover to thoroughly clean your mat. The cleaning methods found on this page are not for the pink Cricut Fabric Grip mat. They are for blue, green, and purple Cricut mats. Don't put anything wet (including water) on your pink fabric mats.

What Is Adhesive Remover?

Adhesive removers are strong solvents that will dissolve some of the adhesive (the sticky glue) on your mat, helping you remove all the gunk that is stuck to it.

Warning: This process will strip your cutting mat of adhesive, so you may have to reapply adhesive to restick your mat. Don't worry, I'll walk you through it.

Which Adhesive Remover Should You Use?

I recommend using Goo Gone as it has been repeatedly and reliably used by the Cricut and crafting community. But you don't need to buy a whole new product for this! If you have any sort of adhesive remover lying around that you're comfortable with, it will likely work just fine. Other options are:

- 70% Isopropyl (rubbing) alcohol
- De-Solv-it Universal Stain Remover & Pre-Wash
- LA's Awesome All Purpose Concentrated Cleaner
- How to use an adhesive remover to clean your Cricut mat
- Read the directions of your adhesive remover, and adapt as necessary.
- Pour or spray a small amount onto your mat.
- Spread it around with a scraper, or any stiff piece of plastic like an old credit card.
- Let the solvent sit and work its magic. The longer you let the adhesive remover sit, the more stuff it will remove. The exact duration will depend on which solvent you use, so read the directions on your bottle.
- Use your scraper to scrape the dirty adhesive off your mat. You can also wipe it off with a cloth or paper towels.
- Wash with soap and warm water to remove any leftover residue.
- Let the mat dry completely.

How Do I Clean My Explore Machine?

Over time, and with use, your machine may collect dust or paper particles, or you may see some of the greases from the machine begin to build upon the carriage track. Cleaning it is easy! Consider the following tips when cleaning your Explore machine:

- Always disconnect the machine from power before cleaning it.
- The machine itself can be cleaned using glass cleaner sprayed on a soft clean cloth.
- If you observe static electricity build-up causing dust or paper particles to accumulate, you can simply wipe that away with a clean soft cloth.
- If you see a buildup of grease on the bar across which the carriage travels, you can use a cotton swab, tissue, or a soft cloth and gently remove it.

Important: Never use any kind of acetone, such as nail polish remover, as that will permanently damage the plastic surfaces of the machine.

Grease Application Instructions

- Turn off the Cricut Explore machine.
- Move the Cut Smart carriage by pushing it slowly to the left.
- Clean the Cut Smart carriage bar with a tissue, wiping around the entire bar (the carriage bar is the one the Cut Smart carriage slides on, just in front of the belt).
- Move the Cut Smart carriage by pushing it slowly to the right.
- Repeat the process of cleaning the Cut Smart carriage bar with a tissue, wiping around the entire bar.
- Slowly move the Cut Smart carriage to the center of the machine.
- Open the lubrication packet and squeeze a small amount of grease onto the end of the cotton swab.
- On both sides of the Cut Smart carriage, apply a light coating of grease around the bar to form a ¼" ring on each side of the carriage.

- Slowly move the Cut Smart carriage to the left and then to the right to distribute the grease evenly along the entire bar.
- Wipe off any grease buildup at the ends of the bar.

Note: If your Explore machine is making a grinding noise, you can request a Grease Packet to be sent (US/Canada only) by contacting our Member Care team.

Important: Keep out of the reach of children. This product may irritate the skin or eyes. In the event of contact with skin or eyes, immediately rinse thoroughly with water and seek medical care if necessary. Wash hands thoroughly after handling.

Tips For Taking Care Of Your Cutting Mats

If you take good care of your cutting mats, they'll take good care of you, and your wallet. Here are some general care tips for your Cricut cutting mats:

1. **Cover Your Mats When Not In Use.**

Keep the clear film cover that came with your cutting mat, and replace the cover as soon as you are done using it. This will prevent dust, hairs, and fibers from accumulating on the sticky surface of the mat. It may help to take a sharpie and mark "TOP" on the top side of the clear acetate cover, so it's easy to replace correctly.

2. **Don't Manhandle Your Mats.**

Avoid excessively touching the sticky surface of the mat with your hands, as this can wear away and damage the adhesive over time. (This is especially true for Cricut's pink fabric mats!) Use the proper tools: spatulas, tweezers, and scrapers to remove cuts and scraps from your cutting mat. This will protect your mats, as well as prevent your finished cut projects from curling and tearing. When you do need to touch your mats, use clean, dry hands that are free of lotion.

3. **Regularly Clean Your Mat.**

Get into the habit of using a sticky lint roller and baby wipes to clean the surface of your cutting mats. This will keep them clean and fresh for each project.

Tips For Drying Cutting Mats

- ❖ Let your mat dry completely by hanging it up, or simply setting it upright in your dish rack. After you've washed it, you want to make sure both sides can get dry, so don't just leave it sitting on your counter.
- ❖ Do not use heat, as heat may cause your cutting mat to split or warp, making it no longer fit in your cutting machine. This means no hairdryers!
- ❖ If you need to speed up the drying time, you can aim a fan at your mat to increase air circulation. I suppose using a hairdryer on the "Cool" setting should be fine, as long as you can trust yourself to not use any heat to speed up the process. No use destroying your last mat just to get a job finished faster! (Though I think you should always have a couple of extra mats around.)

CHAPTER 2: BEST SOFTWARE TO USE WITH CRICUIT EXPLORE AIR MACHINE

What Is The Best Software To Use With Cricut?

1. Adobe Illustrator

No type of graphics design can be discussed without mentioning one of the best tools in the trade. Adobe Illustrator is a vector-based image editor that allows you to create pretty much anything that has shape or color. In the case of Cricut designs, this means being able to create complex and beautiful patterns, and that is something that Adobe Illustrator can do without much effort.

The expanded toolset allows you to create models that are both precise and intricate, and the file formats are perfectly compatible with Cricut hardware. More so, once you are done designing your Cricut patterns, you should know that the software tool can be used for pretty much anything else, as it is not a program with a singular purpose. Let's quickly look at its key features:

- Great for creating intricate and precise patterns
- File formats supported by a wide range of hardware and software
- Its popularity makes it so that tutorials and guides are not hard to find
- The toolset can be further expanded using plug-ins
- Can be tested for free

2. Adobe Photoshop

The world's best imaging and graphic design software need little or no introduction at all, so we're going to jump straight to it. Just like Illustrator, this amazing tool can be paired with your Cricut machine to achieve sophisticated patterns executed with supreme precision. And just like its vector-based sibling, Photoshop is a hugely versatile software that can be used to create pretty much anything your imagination can conceive.

Needless to say that such powerful features cannot be confined to a singular platform or workspace and that is precisely why you can use Photoshop whenever your Cricut inspiration strikes. From PC to mobile workstations, your progress will be instantly updated across all platforms. Since so many artists all around the globe are already used to working in Photoshop, creating Cricut files is rather straightforward and comfortable, we may add.

Just open Adobe Photoshop, then click on Place Embed to add all the PNGs (or other file formats) you want. Then start making use of the powerful editing toolset to resize, rearrange, adjust, add layers, group images, and much more until you are perfectly satisfied with the result. Eliminate the white background (more tools are available for this task – don't be afraid to explore them at your own pace). Once you're satisfied with the outcome, go to the File menu, name your project and choose to save it as PNG. Finally, upload your design in the Cricut tool and you're all set. Let's quickly look at its key features:

- Robust editing toolkit (crop, combine, retouch, resize images to perfection)
- Cross-platform integration (from desktop to mobile station)
- Fully compatible with touch and pen technology
- Unlimited layers, masks, filters, and brushes

- Your work is automatically saved to the cloud
- Adobe Fonts integration to automatically detect all missing fonts
- Object Selection tool to create fast and precise selections

3. Cricut Design Space

Design Space is cloud-based design software that is both easy to learn and lightweight. Use it whenever inspiration strikes and take advantage of its cross-platform compatibility that stretches from laptop to Mac, iOs, and Android devices. You can even use it offline! So what's there not to like?

Let's quickly look at its key features:

- Extensive assets library (images, fonts, pre-made templates, and more)
- Advanced editing toolkit to personalize your project
- Create complex details with unmatched precision
- Step-by-step tutorials and instructional videos
- Extended chat and phone support

4. CorelDRAW

CorelDRAW Graphics Suite is one amazing all-in-one graphic design software to meet every single one of your needs. From apparel and textiles to blueprints and maps and all way to sophisticated illustrations, this feature-rich design suite delivers all the tools you need to conceptualize your ideas and take them one step closer to materialization.

If you've simply outgrown your cartridge collection, it's time to take your Cricut skills up a notch and invest in performant design software that is perfectly adapted for Cricut Machines such as CorelDRAW. This vector-based tool is preferred by many professional cutters who enjoy its complex functionalities, but home cutter crafters will enjoy it just the same. With beautiful typography, support for TTF files, and seamless integration with popular plugins for cutting, CorelDRAW is a great solution to use with your Cricut.

5. Silhouette Software

The final product on our list is not a standalone software, but an already built-in solution meant to facilitate the design process for you. Indeed, some cutters come with full-featured design software and Silhouette Studio is such a tool that allows you to create designs and send them to a Silhouette machine.

As far as we are concerned, the tool does a pretty good job at meeting your basic needs by allowing you to import, customize, and create cutting files. However, if you want to export your work in formats that can be used with other cutters, you will need to adhere to a subscription plan. The premium versions of this software are Designer Edition, Designer Edition +, and Business Edition. To make the most out of your Cricut die-cutting unit, we strongly recommend that you consider these fantastic design software apps that are compatible with Windows systems.

Pair them up with some amazing photo editors or with some 2D digital pixel art tools for the best experience possible. No matter which one you decide to use, you will be able to take control of your creativity, and you'll finally manage to use the Cricut die-cutting system the way that you always wanted to.

Pros

- Works well with a wide array of file formats
- Delivers potent and uniquely helpful editing tools
- Highly compatible with Cricut and other die-cutting machines
- Merges well with other crafting & editing applications

Cons

- Some functions are paid only
- Installing & activating can be tricky

6. Sure Cuts A Lot

This is the most popular option behind Cricut Design Space. And it happens because it works well with a wide array of Cricut machines, going from the Cricut standard to the Silhouette, the Craft ROBO, and even the Wishblade – among many others. You will have the chance to draw, design, color, and edit all kinds of stuff so you can create the most interesting drawings. At the same time, it offers the chance to transform random images into die-cut designs, for even better results no matter what you're looking for. Sure enough, Sure Cuts a Lot is also a piece of cake to use and delivers excellent features that you won't find in other programs. Here's a better idea of the different functions and benefits that Sure Cuts a Lot offers:

- Easy Operation
- High Compatibility
- Extra Plugins & Functions

Pros

- Offers total control of the designs & interface
- Works well with most die-cutting machines & computers

- Updates automatically with complete support
- Offers tons of plugins and extra features

Cons

- Some features may not be compatible with Mac computers
- Only allows one project at a time

7. Make The Cut

Another third-party software system you can use to edit die-cutting designs is Make the Cut or MTC. It offers precisely what Cricut Design Space offers, going from maximum design features to excellent compatibility with most machines. From editing shapes and coming up with unique designs to adding exciting effects and even marking the Cricut pattern – Make the Cut offers it all. But the real advantage comes from its capacity to work with a wide array of files. So it does not only offer the chance to enjoy excellent editing but also unbeatable compatibility. Another advantage is how long it's been in the market – making it a hugely prestigious and reliable option to have. Want to have a more in-depth idea of what it offers? Here are some of its features:

- Convenient Editing
- Next-Level Compatibility
- Fast and Well-Made

Pros

- Fully-equipped editing with tons of features
- Compatible with most die-cutting machines
- Superb file format compatibility
- Reliable and fast system

Cons

- ❖ Not compatible with Cricut machines
- ❖ Faulty compatibility with Mac computers

8. Inkscape

In contrast with the two previous apps, Inkscape is an open-source program. That means you can get it for free, and it will deliver all the best features at no cost. That means you get everything from object creation and manipulation like drawing, cloning, layering, and transforming, to rendering, importing, and exporting files with maximum support. There's a unique vector path system as well, the capacity to create logos, charts, lines, text designs, and even import the most elaborate pieces of art to edit them. And being an open-source program, you can expect it to have excellent support in every way, as well as tons of tutorials and guides to follow when necessary. There's a lot you get with Inkscape, so we decided to summarize it for you:

- ❖ Powerful Editing
- ❖ Outstanding Import & Export
- ❖ Best Compatibility

Pros

- ❖ Works with almost all design file formats
- ❖ Compatible with Linux, Windows, and macOS
- ❖ Won't cost you a single dime to use

Cons

- Editor tends to lag in large projects
- Slightly complex interface.

Cricut Explore Air 2 Project Ideas

How to Make a Customized Graphic T-Shirt

Want to learn how to make T-shirts with Cricut? In this tutorial, we'll make a Cricut iron-on T-shirt, step by step. It might sound intimidating, but using Cricut for T-shirts is simple, once you know where to start. So start brainstorming ideas, and let's dig right into custom T-shirts with Cricut.

What You'll Need For Making T-Shirts With Cricut:

- A design for your shirt
- Cricut explore air or cricut maker
- Iron or cricut easy press
- Iron-on vinyl material
- T-shirt
- Weeding tool

Try to make your design simple if this is your first time making a Cricut iron-on T-shirt. The more complex a design is, the harder time you'll have later in the process.

For this, you can use the Cricut Explore Air or Cricut Maker. We'll be using this for the process of cutting the iron-on vinyl material in the shape of our design. For iron-on vinyl, you have a lot of choices when making T-shirts with Cricut. You can find iron-on vinyl in the crafts section of your local arts and crafts store. Cricut has its brand, but there are many other choices too that will work too. You'll want to keep in mind the color and texture of the material when it comes to your design. Try to pick a color and finish that will match the aesthetics of your design. Using Cricut to make T-shirts can be a lot of fun because there are just so many options. For your Cricut shirts, I would suggest going with 100% cotton. You can find plain T-shirts in most clothing stores, and you can even find plenty of plain shirts at your local arts and crafts store.

Now, let's dig into how to make T-shirts with Cricut.

How To Use A Cricut Machine To Make T-Shirts

Step 1

First, open up Cricut Design Space. Cricut Design Space is free software that comes with your Cricut machine, and it's the first step in learning how to make shirts with Cricut. Once open, you will need to start a new project. You can start a New Project by clicking the New Project button on the top right or the bottom left.

Step 2

Next, we will need to select a template. Templates will let us get a feel for our design and ensure we are creating a print that's the correct size. Select Templates from the sidebar on the left of your Canvas space.

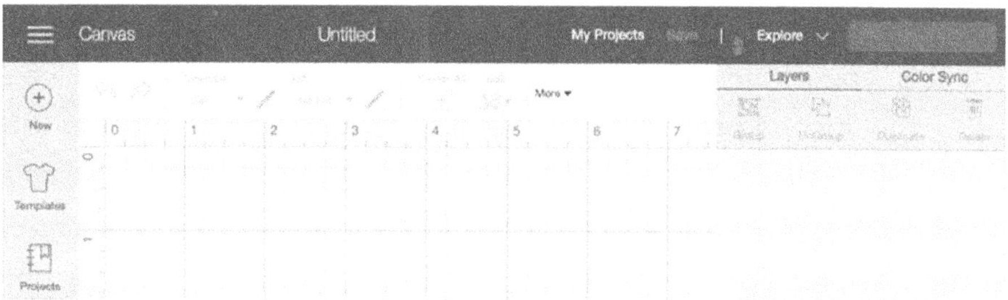

Step 3

Use the search bar to search for a T-Shirt.

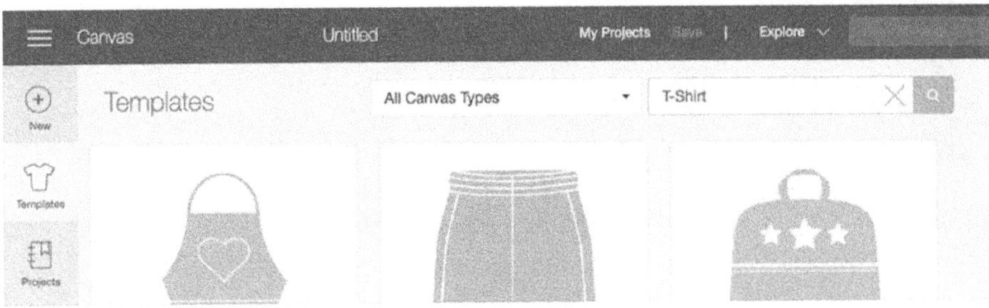

Step 4

From here, select Classic t-shirts. There are many other T-shirt options too. In our case, we want to simply place a graphic in the middle of the chest area, so the specific T-shirt template you use won't matter too much. This will be mostly used for gauging the size of our print.

Step 5

Next, we will upload our design to Cricut Design Space. Again, this software is a vital part of using Cricut to make T-shirts. From the left column, go ahead and click the Upload icon.

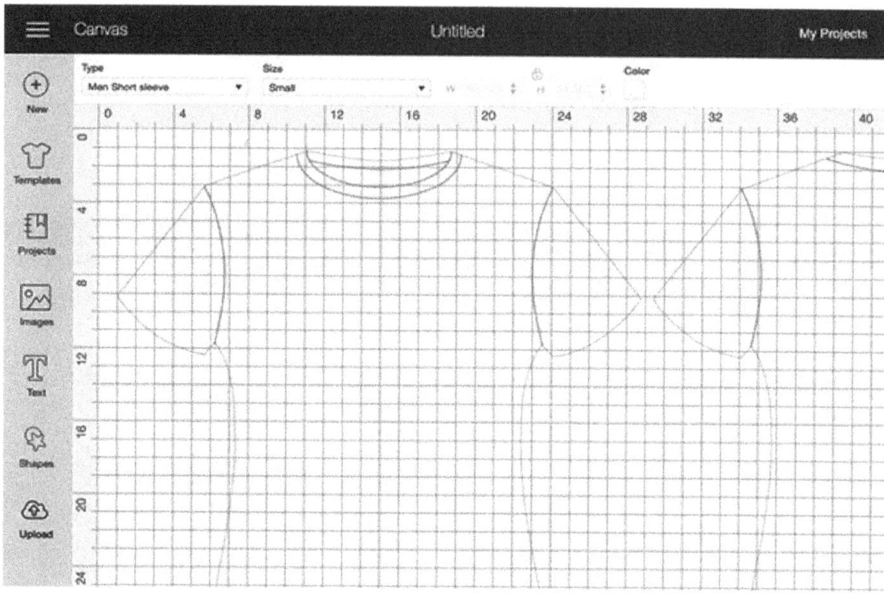

Step 6

As you can see, you're given two choices here. We'll want to use the image type. Cricut Design Space can accept a wide variety of media types. In our case, we are going to be using a transparent PNG file that we created in Photoshop. The key to creating a good cutting image is ensuring that the background is transparent or has a high-contrast background and foreground. Go ahead and click the Upload Image button on the left.

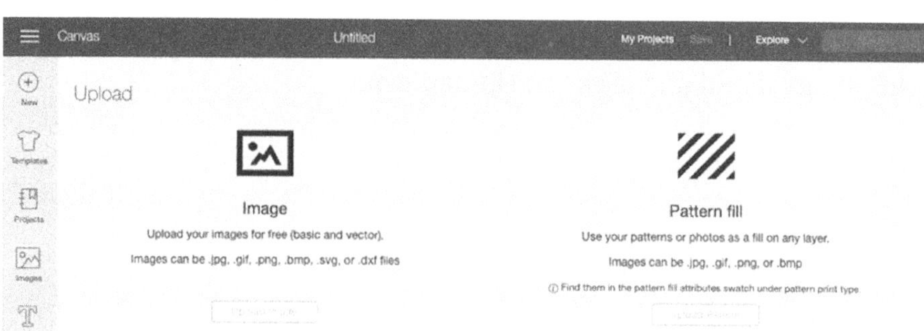

Step 7

From here, you can insert your design. Cricut Design Space accepts .PNG, .JPG, .GIF, .SVG, .DXF, and .BMP file types. I suggest using the SVG file type as this is a great option for large files. It will retain its shape well, regardless of how much we change its dimensions once we import it into the Design Space. You can get your artwork either by dragging your file onto this space or by clicking Browse and selecting your file that way.

Step 8

I went ahead and clicked Browse. Navigate your folders to find the image. In this case, we are picking our SVG typography design.

Step 9

If you've selected an SVG file, this part is relatively straightforward. You can give the image a name and add tags. This is purely for your organizational purposes. As you can see, our design is composed of text and single flat color. We do this to ensure that it's a good match for cutting. Also, we want the start to be the material we picked for our iron-on vinyl. Select Save to add this to your images.

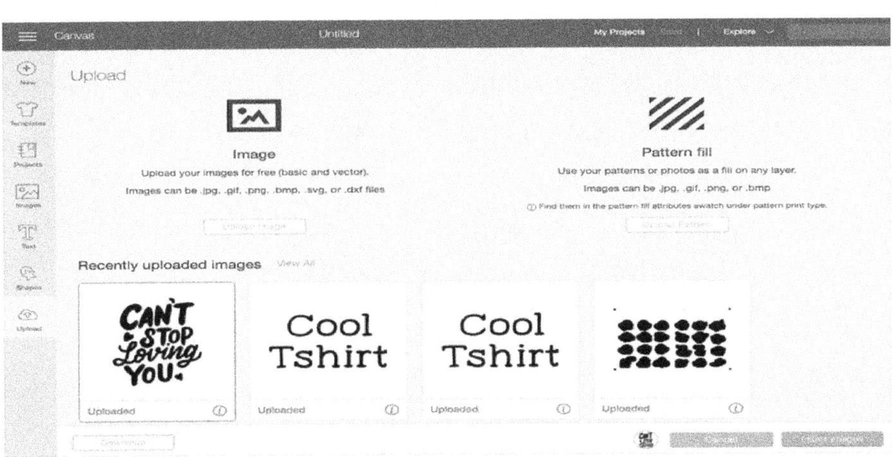

Note For Those Using Different File Types

If you've used a PNG or other file types that aren't an SVG, you will have to do a little more work to prep your cut image for Design Space. (If you're using an SVG file, you can skip down to the next step!)

For PNG images or other types, we are now given various options. Select the Simple setting on the right, and then click Continue on the bottom right. For this step, you can use the Cricut Design Spaces tools to remove the background area. In our case, we already have a transparent image, so we can just go ahead to the next step. Click Continue on the bottom right. Now we get to choose the type of image this is. For our project, we only need to cut it. Go ahead and select Save as a Cut Image.

Step 10

Now you should receive a message that your image was uploaded successfully. It will now join your gallery of images. You should now see your image under Recently uploaded images. Go ahead and select your image. Then click Insert Images on the bottom right.

Step 11

Now your image should be on your stage along with your T-shirt template. From here, arrange your design so it is placed where you want it on the shirt. Click and drag the image to position it.

Step 12

Note that the most important thing here is the scale. We'll be manually ironing this design onto our T-shirts. You can use the icon on the bottom right of your image to scale it.

Step 13

Now, before we make it, we need to ensure that our layers are cleaned up. Ensure that all of your cut images are present here. Depending on how you set up your image, you may have a single image or many different cuts. In my case, I want to cut the shape as I see it here, so let's merge all these cuts. To do so, right-click the layer group and select Weld.

Step 14

Once you're happy with your position and scaling, go ahead and select Make It on the top right.

Step 15

Now that we're on this screen, we can see a preview of what our cut shape will look like. We will have to place our vinyl onto the board. Very Important! Make sure that you select the Mirror option. If you do not select Mirror, then your designs will be printed backward onto your shirt. This is especially true if you have words in your design! Go ahead and select the Mirror Option.

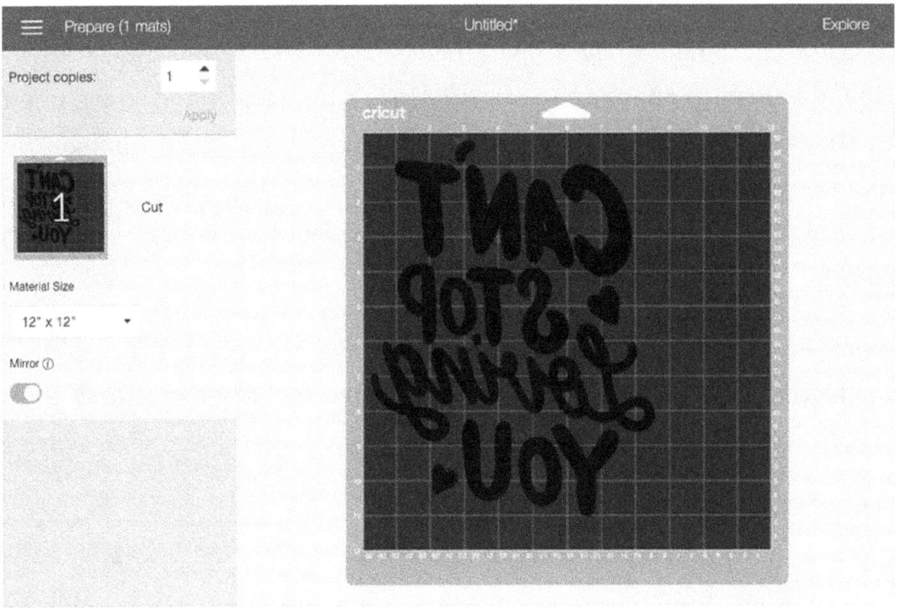

Step 16

Now click Continue on the bottom right.

Step 17

Make sure your Cricut Machine is plugged in and the USB cable is connected to your desktop. You'll now see this screen! Once your Cricut is connected, you'll be given options for the material.

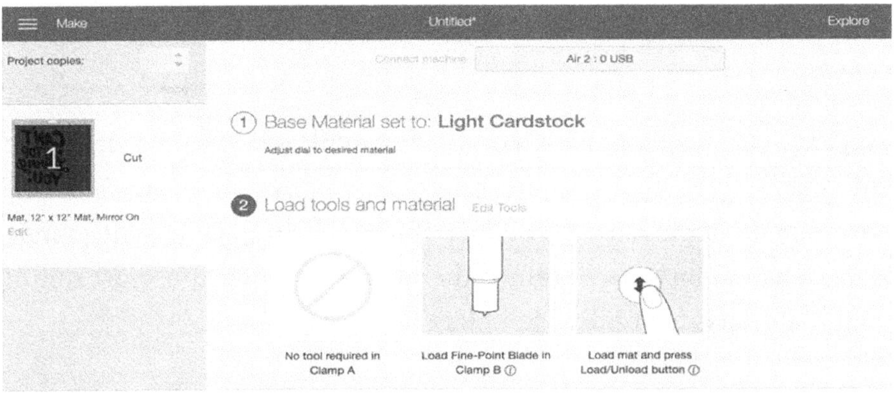

Step 18

Now we need to change the material. We'll be using vinyl, so we need to change it to that setting. Time to enter the real world! Change the dial on your Cricut machine to your desired material, and it will also update in Cricut Design Space. It feels kind of magical for some reason!

Note For Cricut Maker Users: You'll have to select the material through Cricut Design Space. Select Expanded Materials and then select Iron-On.

How To Make Stickers With Cricut

You will also need:

- Printer
- Cricut Design Space app installed on a laptop, PC, tablet, or mobile device
- Printable sticker paper or printable vinyl (I used vinyl)
- Scissors or paper trimmer (optional, to trim down your sticker sheet)

Step 1

Start by opening up the Cricut Design Space app and starting a new canvas.

You can either upload your designs for print and cut, find print and cut images in the image library, or create your own in Design Space by flattening multiple layers together. Print and cut have a print margin of 6.75 x 9.25 inches, therefore the best way to get the most out of your material is to create a template to work on.

To do this, take a square from the shapes library and resize it to 6.75 x 9.25 inches. Then arrange your stickers onto this template, Once you have everything in place, remove the square from the canvas, then select all of the images on the sheet and attach them; this will keep them in place as you move to print and cutting your material.

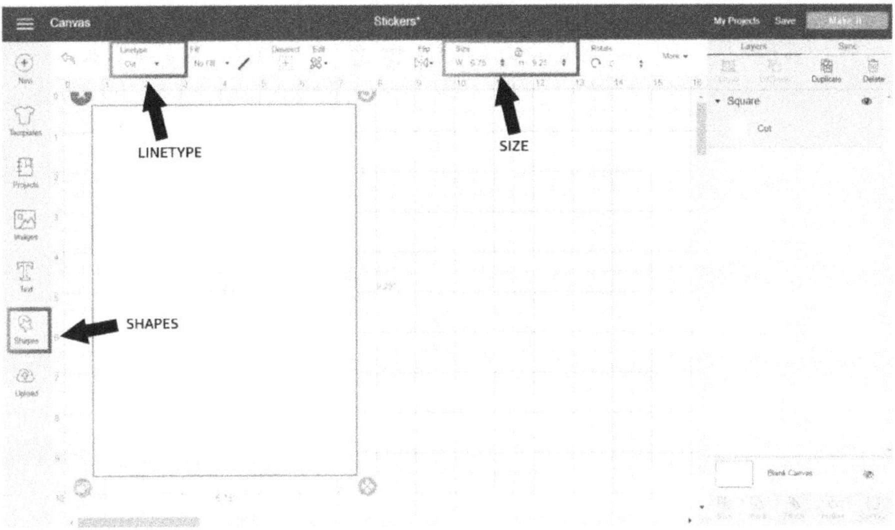

Step 2

Next, click 'Make It'. You will see that your design has been placed inside a lined black box. This black box will be printed and read by the sensors on your machine so that it knows exactly where to cut. Select your machine as usual, then click "Print". This will open up the print screen. Here you have the option to add or remove bleed. This puts a margin around each sticker.

You can also turn on "Use System Dialogue". This will allow you to access your printer's settings.

You can then change any settings for optimal print quality.

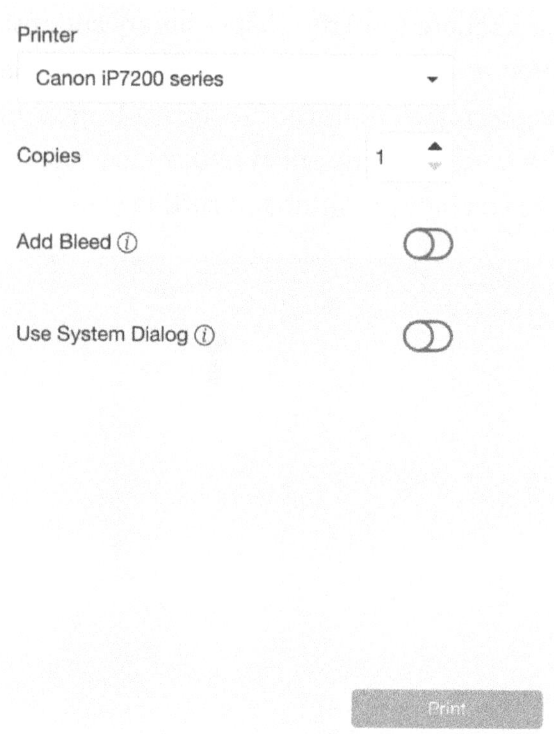

Step 3

Load your printer with your chosen printable material. Check your printer as to whether this needs to be loaded face up or face down, depending on how your printer feeds the paper, then press print.

Step 4

Once the sheet has been printed, place it onto a LightGrip cutting mat, lining it up with the top left-hand corner.

Step 5

Select the material you would like to cut; this is where you tell the machine to make stickers rather than cutting through a material.

Choose the setting for the type of printable material you are using. Then load the mat into the machine. The machine will use its sensors to read the black lines before cutting.

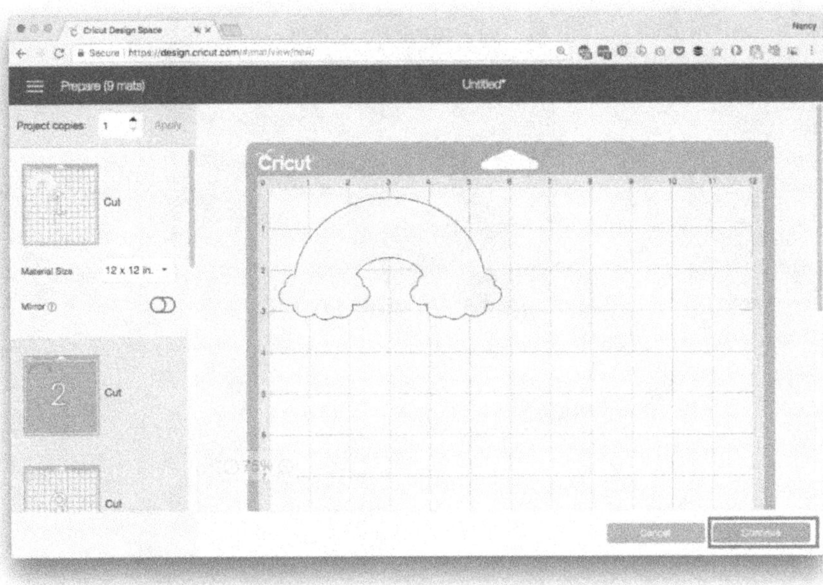

Top Tip: If for any reason, it cannot detect the lines, you need to either move your machine to a darker place or shine a torch onto the sensor lines as the machine reads them.

Once read, the machine will start cutting your stickers.

Step 6

Once cut, the only thing left to do is peel off your stickers and stick them wherever you fancy!

Paper Succulent Template: How To Make Paper Succulent Flowers

Supplies

- Paper succulent templates
- Glue gun
- Scissors
- Cricut Explore
- Wood dowel
- Distress ink and ink sponges
- Floral wire

Step 1

Begin by cutting out all your petal layers. I use six different petal sizes – 2 of each for every flower. You will, therefore, have 12 petal layers per succulent. Cutting machine measurements are as follows:

- 1st (largest petal) – 3 x 3 inches
- 2nd – 2.5 x 2.5 inches
- 3rd – 2.2 x 2.2 inches
- 4th – 2 x 2 inches
- 5th – 1.6 x 1.6 inches
- 6th – 1.3 x 1.3 inches

Step 2

Fold all the petal points up; this is going to give the succulent depth. You can try to make it, so all the petals flow in the same direction for a cleaner look.

Step 3

The next step is to begin layering. Start with gluing your 2 most giant petals on top of another by adding glue to the center. Try not to stack them directly but have the petal alternate, as shown in the 4th block above.

Step 4

You will continue adding in the remaining ten succulent petal layers until you reach the middle. When you get to the very last tiniest petal layer, try to curl the petals around each other a bit and pinch the bottom before gluing in for a more closed center. You can use a thin wood dowel for curling if you want to.

Step 5

Enjoy your lush beauty

How To Make Fabric Bookmark Using Your Cricut Machine?

Supplies:

- Heat N Bond Ultra (for no-sew)
- Heat N Bond Lite (you can sew right over this)
- Fabric
- Design Space Project (this links to the cactus and llama bookmarks pictured.)
- Fray Check
- Cricut Easy Press or Iron

Instructions:

Cut a square of fabric to fit your pink fabric cutting mat. Cut a piece of Heat N Bond that is half the width of the square. Press in place.

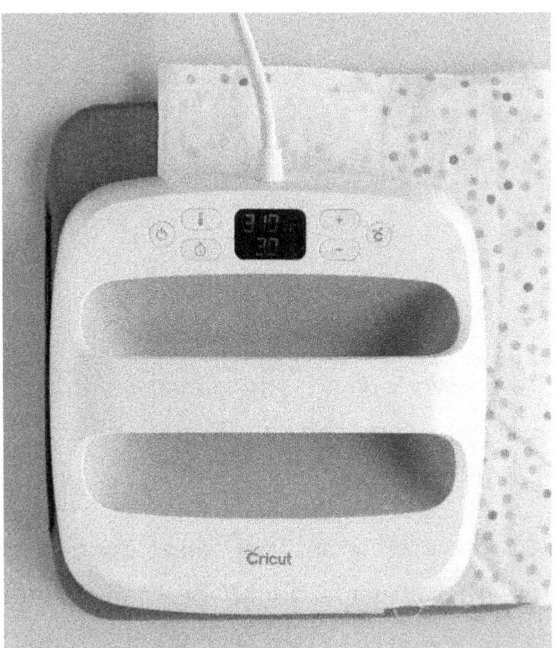

Heat N Bond is meant to be peeled cold, wait for it to cool so the adhesive can set before you try and peel the paper. Peel the paper from the Heat N Bond. Then fold the fabric over and press it in place. Again wait until it has cooled before manipulating the fabric in any way.

Place the fabric onto your pink fabric mat. Use a brayer or rolling pin to press the fabric firmly into the mat. This is especially true if you are using a mat that isn't brand new (as I did!!)

When setting up the cutting settings select bonded cotton as your material, change the pressure to MORE, and change the cutting device to rotary cutter (unless you have a bonded fabric blade.) Cut!

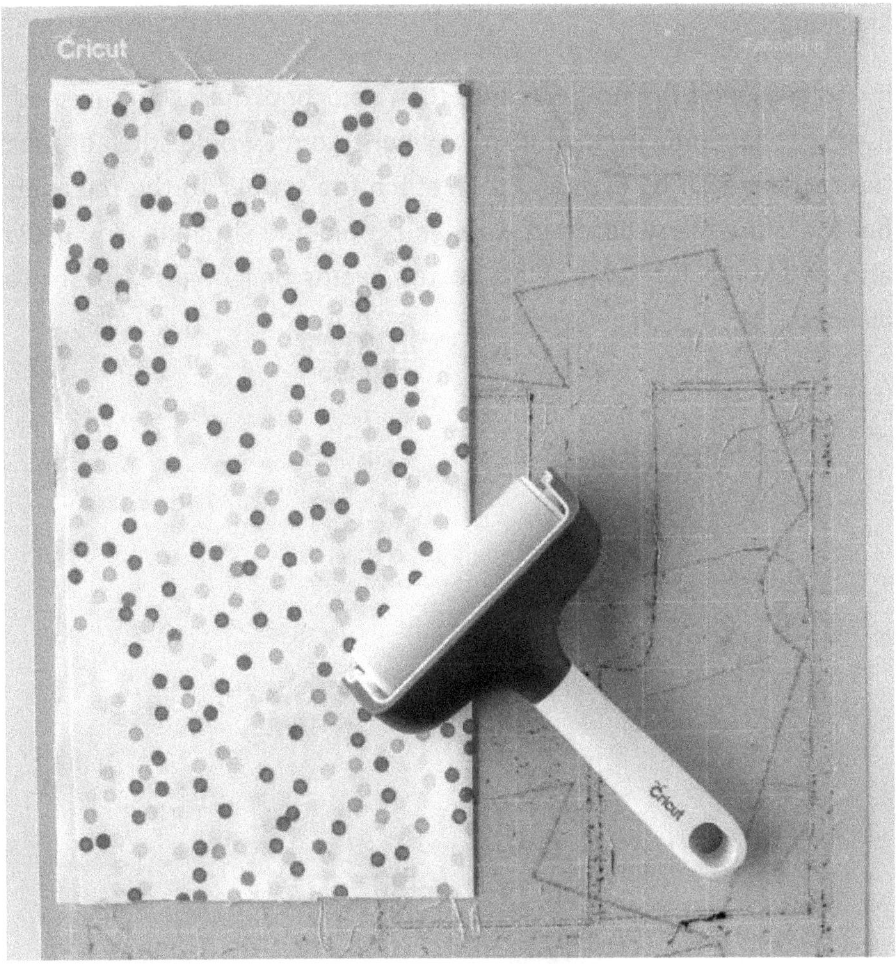

Once you have removed the pieces from the mat you might need to clean the edges up with scissors. I like to give it one more press with my heat source to be sure that all the edges have firmly adhered (but this is probably overkill so you decide!) Then hit the edges with fray check to keep them from fraying, it will also give it a bit more stability as the fray check tends to harden the fabric a bit.

Use your favorite fabric glue to attach the two pieces. I opted for hot glue but any fabric glue should work.

Finishing:

If you are going the no-sew route then your bookmarks are finished! If you are stitching them you know what to do! I would stitch around the rectangle on its own and then stitch the topper to the rectangle but there are many different ways you could add stitching. You could also add some fun embroidery to the cactus or llama if you are so inclined.

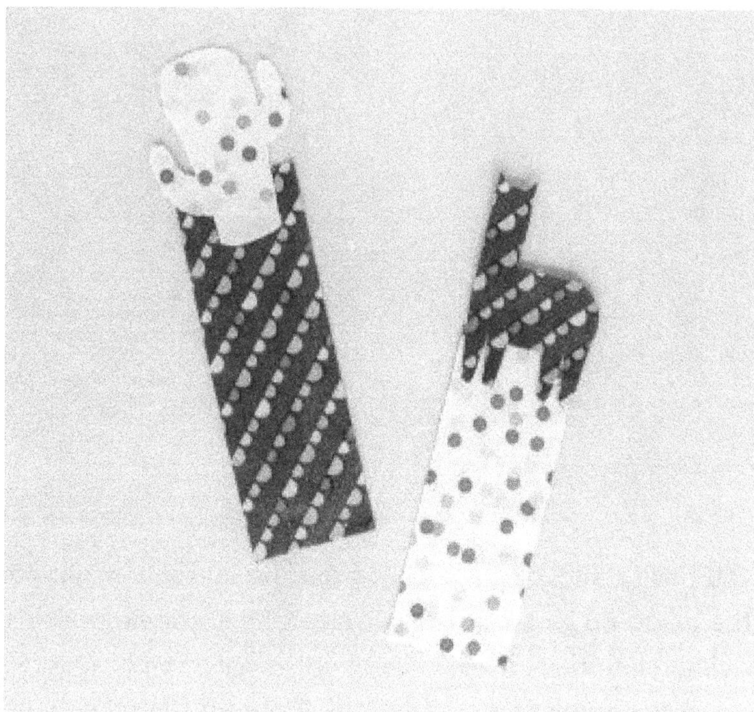

How To Make A Frosted Wreath?

Here's what I used to make my Frosty Wreath:

- Cricut Maker
- Cricut Knife Blade and Rotary Blade Accessories
- strong grip and FabricGrip cutting mats
- Cricut Chipboard
- Cricut Felt
- Vine Wreath
- Premium Vinyl – Permanent Silver
- Fabric Brayer
- Masking Tape

❖ Glue

For this wreath, I used a design I worked up in Cricut Design Space.

The size of the design elements is set for an 8" wreath. You can customize it to enlarge or shrink the elements depending on your wreath size, up to 10.5 inches. Chipboard projects cannot be bigger than 10.5 x 10.5.

There are several tips you should pay close attention to when working with Cricut Chipboard, or other thick knife-cut materials. I'm happy to share them with you here:

Make sure you've pushed the star wheels on the machine to the side.

The star wheels are the little white wheels in front of the blade that help to pull materials through when cutting. But with the thicker materials, the star blades will just leave track marks on the chipboard or wood. So be sure they aren't running over your design while cutting!

Let the chipboard acclimate out of the package for 24 hours before using. If it starts to bend or warp place a flat heavy object on top of it.

The knife blade can cut designs bigger than .75" and smaller than 10.5". Super intricate images can damage the blade so it's best to keep knife cuts on the somewhat simple side. You can see that my snowflakes worked out ok. The small snowflake has nice straight edges.

Use a Brayer to smooth the chipboard onto a StrongGrip cutting mat to make sure the chipboard has adhered nicely and then use masking tape or blue painters tape to tape around the edges, securing the chipboard (or wood piece) securely to the mat.

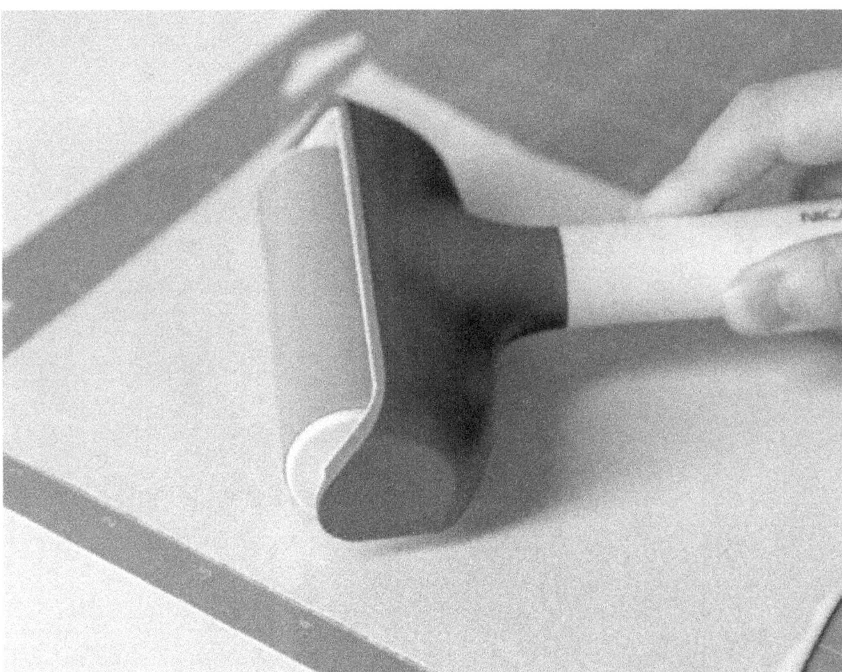

Check your machine's cutting progress frequently. The Maker is set to make 20 passes when cutting heavy Chipboard, but in the case of my "Frosty" word art it only took 12, and it only took 8 passes on the big snowflake. Pause the machine frequently and lift the edge of the chipboard to check the progress.

If the design is cut through most of the way, remove it from the mat and use a knife tool to cut through the rest. This will save your StrongGrip cutting mat from extra wear.

Expect some cut lines and wear on your cutting mat. With the amount of pressure the Maker is using and the sharpness of the knife blade it is unavoidable. You can minimize the mat damage by keeping a close eye on your cut. Each design will cut differently depending on the simplicity, or complexity of the cuts and the materials being used.

Before cutting the word "Frosty out, put some Silver Permanent Premium Vinyl on the Heavy Chipboard.

It worked out ok to cut the chipboard with the vinyl adhered already, and then you don't have to worry about lining the vinyl up after the cuts.

Load the chipboard into the machine on the Strong Grip mat, and press Go! Watch the knife blade do all the hard work. I was impressed by the ability to cut the snowflake out of the letter O! Keep a close eye on the cut progress, pause the cut anytime you need to remove a piece of chipboard that has broken loose. I found the most pieces coming loose in the snowflakes. It's important to remove the loose pieces before they become stuck and damage the blade.

After 12 passes, Frosty was done! I loaded the second piece of chipboard for my large snowflake. That one took even fewer passes because it was a simpler cut.

When you remove the chipboard, if there are segments that have not been cut all the way through, simply take the knife blade and lightly cut along the lines to free the design.

You can paint the chipboard if you don't want to vinyl it! Just seal it first with a coat of mod podge and you're good to go! I painted my large snowflake with Blue Glitter paint.

To add some dimension to the wreath, I added some felt snowflakes too! To cut the felt snowflakes, I switched to the Rotary Blade that is included with the Maker. Just change the material setting to felt, move the star wheels back into place, and change the tool to the rotary blade and you're all set! Use the Fabric Grip Cutting Mat and the brayer to adhere the felt before cutting.

Faux Leather Bracelet Cricut Tutorial: How To Make It

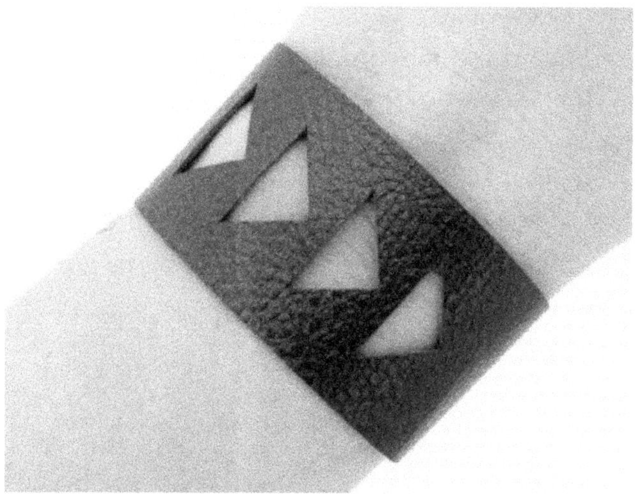

What You Need to Create a Faux Leather Bracelet

- Cricut Faux Leather – Pebbled
- Printable Fabric (for fabric and leather bracelets shown)
- Measuring Tape
- Scissors
- Hot Glue Gun

Design Space Instructions:

Before you start creating the bracelet, measure around your wrist with the Measuring Tape. Make sure it's not too tight.

Open up Cricut Design Space and create a new project.

Select a shape, and click on the square. Press the lock icon to unlock it.

Drag the corner of the square until it is about 1.5" wide, and then the length of your wrist plus 1.5" to 2". So, if your wrist is 6 inches around, your bracelet will be about 8 inches long.

Select the triangle shape, then unlock it. resize it to about 3/4" wide and 1/2" tall. Copy and paste it three times. Align them to the center horizontally, then distribute vertically and click on ATTACH.

Now, align the triangles with the rectangle, vertically and horizontally, then click on ATTACH.

Create two more rectangles, each 1/4" by 2."

Click on the green MAKE IT in the upper right-hand corner, then send it to the Cricut.

Place the Cricut Faux Leather – Pebbled on a mat and use a regular blade to cut it out.

If you want to create a fabric bracelet, cut out the leather without the triangles.

Next, create a new project and upload the bracelet file and resize it to the size of the leather bracelet you just cut out. No need to cut out the small straps again.

Add the rectangles again, and align them the same way.

Weld the triangles together, then align them to the bracelet, then click on ATTACH.

To Assemble The Bracelet:

- Take the rectangles off the mat.
- Hot Glue the end of one of the small rectangles to the back of the bracelet.
- Pull the strap around the top of the bracelet, then glue the other end to the back of the bracelet, as well.
- Repeat with another strip.
- Allow the glue to dry, then cut the sides of the end of the bracelet at an angle. This makes it easier to pull the end through.
- Now you can start wearing it!

How To Make Planner Stickers With Cricut

What I Used:

- Cricut Explore Air 2
- Silhouette Sticker Paper
- Printer
- Free Planner Sticker Printable

Method 1: Using A Printable Sheet

Step 1: Set Up Your File

Upload your printable file to Cricut Design Space using the Upload tab. Select "Complex" as your image type. Delete the background by simply clicking the white space!

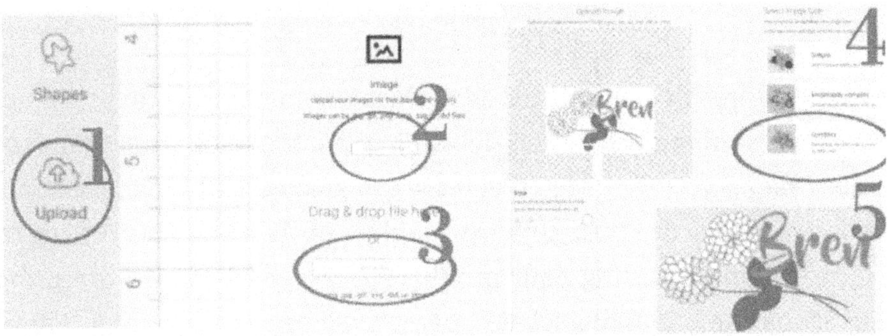

On your CDS canvas click (1)Upload, then (2)Upload Image, (3)browse

Now find your image you have saved on your computer and click it.

Any time you upload an image you will be sent immediately (unless it's an SVG File) to the Upload area where you have to (4) choose Simple, Moderately Complex, or Complex. Then click continue.

Step 2: Load Your Sticker Paper

Load your sticker paper into your printer, making sure that it is facing the correct way. The printer I used let me load my paper facing up, however you may need to flip your paper upside down depending on yours. Test it to make sure.

Step 3: Print

Once your image is uploaded you will click the "Make It" button to print and cut. The largest image that you can use the Print/Cut feature on will be 9.25"x 6.75", so make sure to re-size your image if it is larger than that. Set up and select your printer from the next screen and click Print!

Step 4: Cut

Place your freshly printed sticker sheet onto your cutting mat face-up. Your cut settings will differ depending on the type and brand of sticker paper you are using. If you are using any Cricut brand products you can access the best settings for those by setting your Cricut to "Custom" and selecting your product on-screen. Since we are using the Silhouette brand of sticker paper we will be putting on the "Paper –" setting. Follow the onscreen cues to load your mat and cut your stickers.

Method 2: Design Your Own!

As much as I love printable files, sometimes they lack exactly what it is that you may need to schedule your planner. Creating custom planner stickers is a super easy and useful skill to have to either make your planner that much more personal or to add one more addition to the things that you can make and sell using your Cricut!

Step 1: Text

Once you have your Canvas open, you will want to select your Text tool. Type out whatever it is that you would like your design to say and change the font in the upper left-hand corner of your screen. If your letters seem to bunch together or too far apart, play around with your Letter Space settings to get them on track.

Step 2: Add A Shape

Adding a shape behind your text is the best way to cut out a usable sticker. You can either upload a shape using the print/cut method I showed you earlier OR use one of Cricut's shape tools to make your own! For this example, I chose a heart out of the shape tool menu.

Step 3: Convert To Print

Next, go to your layers menu and select the colors that you would like your design to print. Then make sure to convert your file from a CUT file into a PRINT file by selecting PRINT under your layer attribute window. You can always double-check this by seeing if the icon beside your layer shows a pair of scissors or a printer.

Next, you will want to select both of your layers and select FLATTEN.

This will combine your layers into one flat printable image. From here I re-sized my image to my preferred size and then used the copy/paste function to make a full sheet. Keep in mind the maximum image size that I mentioned earlier when designing your sheet. If you go over this size, Design Space will automatically try to re-arrange your sheet into multiple mats.

Step 4: Print/Cut

Once you have designed your full sticker sheet, simply click the "Make It" button and follow the on-screen instructions exactly like you would for the Printable Sheet shown during the first part of the tutorial.

Step 5: Plan!

This might be the only tutorial that you follow where planning is the last step! Use these stickers to help you plan out the next big thing.

CHAPTER 3: MAKING MONEY WITH CRICUT

Before you get started trying to earn a profit with your Cricut, take some time to think about whether or not it's actually what you want to do. Here are some things to think about:

- Are you doing it just because your friends say your creations are amazing?
- Do you want to support your family?
- Or are you doing it for some play money on the side?
- Are you willing to deal with difficult customers (there are always difficult customers!)?
- Do you want to turn something you love to do into a job?
- Are you tech-savvy enough to set up a basic site or Etsy shop?
- Can you learn more about marketing on and offline?
- Do you have the time and space to start a small business?
- Do you enjoy crafting with your Cricut? Enough to do it over and over again?
- I don't want to deter you from starting to make money with your Cricut, I just want you to be smart about it.

What To Make Or Sell With Circuit

If making things from scratch appeals, the Cricut Maker is one of the best tools available to crafters and DIYers. The Cricut maker is a sophisticated machine that handles many different materials, giving the user the ability to cut them into intricate designs and shapes. A Cricut handles balsa wood, leather, fabric, and paper, among the 300 different materials it can cut with incredible precision. Several add-on tools can be purchased for the Cricut that allow it to handle even more tasks and craft projects.

For the person who loves making crafts and gifts at home, the Cricut maker is one that can be a lot of fun to use. Just imagine being able to take on a new craft project every day and having each different than the last. That's why crafters and DIY fans love the tool so much.

- Tea Towels
- Hand Towels
- Custom Shirts
- Custom Stuffed Animals
- Blankets
- Name Tiles
- Drink Coasters
- Earrings +other jewelry
- Painted Wood Signs
- Vinyl on Wood Signs
- Canvas Art
- Hair Bows
- Key Chains
- Drink Cups
- Tumblers
- Sports Bottles
- Coffee Mugs
- Paper Flowers
- Invitations
- Party Banners
- Garden Flags
- Hats
- Makeup Bags
- Shoes

- Pillows
- Pot Holders
- Wood signs
- Reusable stencils
- Faux leather earrings
- Wine glasses
- Homemade puzzles
- Etched glass
- Fairy Nightlight
- Cake toppers
- Rubber stamps
- Personalized Doormat
- Easy cards
- No-sew hair bows
- Face mask with a window
- Custom letterboards
- Animal shirt
- Fabric buntings
- Monogram necklace
- Terra cotta pots
- Patterned iron-on sea turtle bag
- Craft foam bookmarks
- Sport flex iron-on swimwear
- Leather keychains
- Iron on the pillow cover
- Christmas vinyl décor
- Tropical tray
- Iron on the straw bag
- Wooden painted signs

Saving Money Tips

If you're looking for ways to save money while you craft with your Cricut, look no further! These money-saving tips and tricks are sure to help during your next Cricut project.

Clean And Reuse Your Mats

If you're not already cleaning and resticking your old mats, you absolutely should! If your mat is still a little sticky, you can probably get away with using a baby wipe and then rinsing with a little soap and water.

However, if your mat has lost its sticking power, try using some spray adhesive. Make sure the surface of the mat is clean. Then, tape the edges so they don't get sticky. Grab your spray and cover the surface of the mat. It should be good as new! Here are some adhesive sprays I would recommend:

- Kryolan All-Purpose Spray Adhesive
- 3M General Purpose Spray Adhesive
- Loctite General Performance Spray Adhesive

Use A Pen Adapter

I'm constantly using pens in my Cricut Explore Air to make cards, and those Cricut pens are super pricey!. You put it into the pen slot and it allows you to use TONS of different pens and markers not just the Cricut ones! Now I can use pretty much any pen or marker I want, which saves me lots of money, plus it gives me way more options when I'm making a card!

Keep Vinyl On A Roll

Instead of cutting off a new piece of vinyl every time you go to cut out a new design, try leaving your vinyl on the roll. That way, when you're done with a cut, you can just use some scissors to cut around the used section. This will save you from wasting any precious vinyl.

Use Household Objects As Tools

This one is only limited to your creativity! While you can go out and buy new weeding tools, a lot of the time, things you can find around the house will work just as well.

Invest In An Svg And Font Subscription

This one might sound counter-intuitive, but trust me, it's not!

If you find yourself buying a lot of fonts and SVG files, you might consider a Creative Fabrica subscription. They have a few different plans, but I'll list the 3 big ones here.

- **The Crafter Plan:** For $12 every 3 months and get access to over 17,000 SVG files for commercial use.
- **The Font Plan:** For $15 a month, you get unlimited access to over 15,000 fonts for commercial use.
- **The All-Access Plan:** For $30 a month you get access to all of the fonts, graphics, and SVG files on the site for personal and commercial use.

Order In Bulk

If you've got a vinyl cutting business, your main expenditures are likely blanks and vinyl. Instead of buying these at your local Michaels, you should try ordering wholesale and in bulk. Many stores will give you deep discounts for doing this, so there's a ton of money to be saved

Use Free Svg Files And Fonts

If you're frequently making a lot of different designs and you don't currently have a Creative Fabrica subscription, you can still save money!

Lots of websites and designers offer free SVG files and fonts. Many are for personal use, where you would have to purchase a license if you want to sell any items made using the design, however, some are for free for commercial use!

Check Your Heat Press Energy Consumption

Something that many people don't consider when buying a heat press is the cost of electricity! Commercial heat presses are an industrial appliance, and they often use a ton of power. Many do not come with an auto shut-off timer, which can consume lots of power if you forget to turn it off (not to mention how dangerous that is!).

Vinyl Project Ideas

The options for customizing vinyl are truly endless!! Almost anything you can find with a smooth surface, vinyl will stick to. If you have a project with rough edges like wood, you can use your vinyl as a stencil and paint your design on. I have gathered some great project ideas along with the type of vinyl you should use for these projects. This is just a recommendation so make sure you know the vinyl you are wanting to use. I will recommend the brand and why I like it in this post. Remember this is only a guide and you don't have to follow it if you don't want to. I hope this inspires you and directs you on the right path for your project.

1. Adhesive Vinyl

Adhesive vinyl is a thin, flexible, self-adhesive material (think durable sticker) that is typically used to create wall and window decals and business signage. It's durable and can also be waterproof which makes it very versatile. Adhesive vinyl comes in many forms; glossy, matte, glitter, patterned, metallic, just to name a few.

Adhesive Vinyl

Adhesive vinyl always has a paper backing material. You should be able to peel the vinyl away from the paper and feel the sticky adhesive. If you can't, then it isn't adhesive vinyl. When cutting adhesive vinyl you'll always place the paper backing down against the cutting mat.

The type of adhesive vinyl you use fully depends on the project at hand. If you want to create seasonal chalkboard art or maybe add a decal to the wall inside your home, use removable. If you want to add a monogram to a sand bucket or create a coffee mug, use it permanently! Generally speaking, if it's going to be exposed to heat, water, or any extreme elements, outdoor permanent is the way to go.

Types Of Adhesive Vinyl

When you are trying to decide which vinyl to use for a project, take into account the type of project you are doing. If you're making a tumbler, you'll want it to hold up to washing choose permanent vinyl. If you're doing a decal on a wall that will need to come down at some point, removal vinyl is a better choice.

Permanent / Outdoor Vinyl

Permanent Outdoor Vinyl is the most well known and widely used craft vinyl because of its long-lasting permanent adhesive. The permanent outdoor vinyl is perfect for coffee mugs, water bottles, car decals, and any outdoor application. While it's not truly "permanent" it does last for up to 8 years! Outdoor vinyl typically comes in a glossy finish but there are a few matte options as well . Permanent vinyl is great when you want a lasting stick, like car decals, mugs and tumblers that will be washed, and outdoor signage. In most cases, permanent vinyl will need a solvent to remove the adhesive. Permanent vinyl may be called:

Cricut Permanent Vinyl

1. **Oracal 651:** Glossy and matte (the most popular)

2. **Oracal 641:** Matte (rated for outdoor use, but not as water-resistant as other permanent vinyl

3. **Oracal 751:** Glossy (rated for even longer outdoor use)

Removable Indoor Vinyl

Removable vinyl is perfect for applications where you may want to remove the vinyl in the future. Think wall decals, temporary signs, and decorations, etc. The most removable vinyl adhesive can be removed by just peeling it up. Removable indoor vinyl is great for temporary applications such as wall decals, indoor signs, or chalkboards. It typically has a matte finish.

- Cricut Removable Vinyl
- Cricut Vinyl (older and being discontinued, does not specify permanent or removable)

- Oracal 631: matte

Specialty Adhesive Vinyl

There are other kinds of adhesive vinyl as well! Many of these aren't rated for long-term outdoor use, but you can always read the label to find out the suggested uses. Here are a few types of specialty adhesive vinyl:

- Holographic
- Glitter
- Metallic
- Foil
- Chalkboard
- Dry Erase
- Glow in the Dark
- Patterned
- Printable
- Fluorescent / Neon
- Window Cling

How Is Adhesive Vinyl Different Than Iron-On Vinyl (HTV)?

As mentioned above, adhesive vinyl has a sticky back. Iron-on vinyl (often called heat-transfer vinyl or HTV) has a heat-activated back. Adhesive vinyl applies more like a sticker whereas you'll need a heat source (like an EasyPress, iron, or heat press) for iron-on vinyl. Adhesive vinyl is best for smooth surfaces, like glass, plastic, metal, notebook covers, painted wood (raw wood is harder), and even paper. Iron-on vinyl is primarily used on fabric, so you can use it to make t-shirts, onesies, and more, as well as on raw wood and other hard surfaces that are more porous

What Is Heat Transfer Vinyl?

Heat transfer vinyl is a type of permanent vinyl that can only be applied with heat. Typically it's used on things like shirts, pillowcases, blankets, etc. But you can also use it on wood and glass!. By using a vinyl cutter, like a Silhouette CAMEO or Brother ScanNCut, you can cut digital designs into the vinyl and then transfer those designs onto your T-shirt or garment using a heat press. The result is impressive, high-quality custom garments with exceptional durability as well as look and feel. One of the great things about heat press vinyl is that there are so many different varieties of colors and finishes - glossy, matte, flock, stretchy, glow-in-the-dark, glitter HTV - you name it! No matter what project you've got, there is an HTV that's perfect for it.

How Do You Apply Heat Transfer Vinyl To Your Project Material?

There are three ways you can apply heat transfer vinyl:

1. Heat Press: This is the largest and most expensive (depending on what type you get) option to apply your vinyl. If you have a business or just do a lot of shirts I recommend looking into a heat press because it can do designs up to 15×15 and it's very rare that you'll ever need to make a design bigger than that. You also get even pressure with a heat press, and that's important!

2. Cricut EasyPress: This is similar to a heat press but it is smaller and easier to store if you are limited on space. I use an EasyPress and I love it, though I wish I had waited to get the bigger size (it came out a few months after I bought mine...of course!). Mine is a 9×9 so I have to press my designs multiple times to make sure I've heated all the vinyl. This sometimes causes uneven pressure on the vinyl which you can see if you look close enough.

3. Iron: If shirts are not something you'll make a lot of then iron will be fine. However, depending on how big your design is you'll be pressing it a lot to make sure you are heating every piece of the design. If you are heavy-handed with your pressure one time and not the next, you'll have uneven pressure points on your vinyl. If you look closely you'll see lines in the vinyl design from that pressure. This isn't that big of a deal if the shirt is for you, but if you're making them for other people you don't want those pressure points on your shirts. It can also cause your vinyl to come up off the shirt when you wash it.

Window Cling Vinyl

What Is Window Clings?

Window clings use static electricity (not adhesive like vinyl) to stick to windows- so there is no glue involved. They are made from a rubber-like substance can be cut using a Cricut, Silhouette, or any other die cutting machine into custom shapes. There are also custom printed window clings available on the market from retailers.

How Do Window Clings Work?

Static window clings do not have any sticky material, they rely on static electricity much like how you sometimes notice objects stick to clothes or mirrors due to electric attraction between the positive and negative electrodes. So when you go to cut out and stick on your window clings you will find that the two surfaces naturally tend to be attracted to each other and are held together by static electricity. This imbalance of electrons creates a bond between the two surfaces which allows static cling to stick to mirrors, glass, and other smooth hard surfaces that are capable of carrying an electrical charge.

Do Window Clings Go Inside Or Outside?

Window clings by nature are not permanent, so they are best placed inside. If you place a static cling decal on your car windshield for example it will likely fall off and blow away in the wind after a few short minutes of driving. For this reason, we advise keeping your static window cling film indoors on surfaces such as mirrors and glass. Static cling is a short term option display designs or print outs and is not able to withstand harsh elements such as rain.

What Is Window Clings Made Out Of?

Window cling is made out of thin yet durable vinyl material. It is scratch and tear-resistant, though there is no adhesive gel material involved. Cricut static cling for example comes in a roll with a paper backing and the vinyl static cling material attached to it. It is machine cutter compatible and often comes in a single solid color. It is more difficult to use printable static window cling material, though there are options available on the market.

How Do You Get Window Clings To Stick?

If your window cling is not sticking to the surface the best option is to remove the cling and clean the surface, either with rubbing alcohol or water to remove debris. You can also gently rinse your static cling with warm water and let it dry. This will also encourage both surfaces to recharge the imbalance of electrical charge, allowing the window cling film to re-stick to the surface.

How Long Does Window Cling Last?

Static window cling can last for 1-2 years indoors before the surface needs to be cleaned again. For outdoor use the lifespan is significantly lower, lasting as little as a couple of days in harsh elements such as wind or rain. If the area is commonly disturbed by touching or brushing it frequently, such as a front door or mason jar, the static cling will likely fall off quickly. In this case, we recommend using adhesive vinyl instead of static window cling for a more permanent solution.

FAQS

Troubleshooting

The First Things To Try Before Going Any Further Are:

- Turn your machine off completely, before turning it back on.
- Check the power supply and socket.
- Check for an update on Cricut Design Space.
- Log out of Cricut Design Space then back in.
- Check that nothing is stuck in any part of your machine if so carefully remove it.

Machine

My Machine Isn't Cutting My Material:

Check the stickiness of your mat. Check that you are using the correct colored mat for the material you are cutting. Clean your blade; check for any debris that may be caught around the blade tip. -Use a ball of foil to sharpen your blade, by stabbing it multiple times. If this doesn't work, you may need to consider a new blade. Check that you have the correct setting for the material you are cutting. If you are a Cricut Explore user turn your dial to custom and choose from a wider range of materials there. Increase the blade pressure by changing the material set Increase the image size, the image may be too small and intricate. For intricate cuts on the card, use the intricate cut card setting, for intricate cuts on vinyl try the washi sheets setting.

The Power Button On My Machine Is Red:

Flashing Red Light

My Machine Isn't Registering The Print And Cut Marks:

Make sure the machine is in shade, bright sunlight stops the sensor from picking up the lines, If this doesn't work it might be that your room is too dark! Try shining a torch onto the sensor. The Explore Air Machines can only register white cardstock, The Maker, however, can detect print and cut lines on colored and Kraft card -Go over the black lines with a black sharpie, to help your machine pick up the line.

Print And Cut Aren't Cutting Exactly: Re-calibrate your machine, you may have to do this a few times to get the best results. -Check if a bleed has been enabled

Turn on System Dialogue (underneath bleed on the print screen) this will give you more print options.

Mats

My mats are no longer sticky: Wash with washing up liquid, gently rubbing into the mat surface, rinse in warm water and leave to air dry. Designate mats for certain materials. Buy a new mat!

The material is tearing when I remove it from the mat: Turn over the mat, and peel the mat away from the material. Check that you are using the right colored mat for the right type of material. On the first mat use, press the mat against a piece of clothing to get rid of a little stickiness

Easy Press

My vinyl is not adhering well when using my easy press: Check that the surface you are pressing on is sturdy. Always use the Easy Press mat. Check the correct temperature, and time, for your material and vinyl on the online Easy Press guide. Check the peel off temperature for the vinyl you are using, if it is cold peel wait for it to cool completely before peeling away the carrier sheet.

Which Is The Best Cricut Machine For Beginners?

When it comes to precision crafting and cutting, Cricut machines are revered for their superior power. No matter your level of experience, you can always find a Cricut-branded machine that enables you to put your skills to good use. But with so many options on the market, the task of finding one that best suits your needs might be a little complicated. In fact, as a beginner, you might be tempted to invest in the latest, whizz-bang Cricut machine. However, we'd advise against that. As a beginner, it's always a good idea to test the waters before splurging on the newest machine. So, if you are just getting started, we have curated a list of some of the best machines that are beginner-friendly.

Cricut Explore One

If you are just getting started in crafting and looking for a reliable machine, this is one of the options worth looking into. It looks a lot like the Explore Air 2 but they are not the same. The Explore One was just released as an inexpensive alternative to the Explore Air 2. Compared to the Explore Air 2, Explore One does not have Bluetooth technology. The good news is that you can add a wireless Bluetooth adapter for wireless cutting with your iPhone, PC, iPad, and Mac. However, the adapter is sold separately.

But probably the best thing about the machine is that it can cut a wide array of materials. In particular, you can use it to cut vinyl, paper, leather, fabric, cardstock, and even poster board for DIY projects. On top of that, thanks to its Smart Set dial function, the machine allows you to get precise cuts on almost any material. You can as well design a custom setting for a wide variety of materials. In addition to that, it features unique Cut Smart technology designed to help you make clean cuts of different shapes and sizes.

Moving on, the machine boasts easy-to-use and free Design Space software that is only available online. This software provides you with access to your projects and images from any compatible iPhone, Mac, PC, or iPad. Similarly, the software is cloud-based to ensure your projects and designs are synced across all your devices.

What's more? It includes over 50 free images and 25 one-click projects so you can get started as soon as you purchase the machine. More so, you can upload your personalized images and fonts for free or simply choose from the image library. You also have the option to browse pre-made projects for cards, home decor, scrapbook pages, parties, and more to satisfy your crafting needs.

Pros

- Makes ultra-precise cutting
- Includes over 60,000 design and projects ideas
- Cuts over 100 different types of materials including printable images

- No complex material settings thanks to the Smart-set dial
- Relatively inexpensive and works with Design Space
- Easy to use and comes with an instruction guide
- Allows you to design your projects on your smartphone, PC, or tablet

Cons

- Not embedded with Bluetooth so you will need to buy an adapter
- Includes just a single holder so you cannot cut and write simultaneously
- Cartridges are quite expensive

Cricut Explore Air

The Explore Air is yet another great entry-level Cricut machine for beginners that allows for customized designs. It includes everything you might need to create stunning DIY projects and crafts. Like the Explore One, it also cuts a wide variety of materials with superb accuracy. From thick fabrics like leather to paper, adhesive vinyl, vellum, and even iron-on, it precisely cuts over 60 types of materials.

Unlike the Explore One, this machine has a dual carriage including one for a cutter and the other one for a marker. This means that it can easily cut a card and write a customized message on the card in one step. Also, it can cut a box and then score its fold lines simultaneously. Similarly, the dual tool holder helps keep your pen and blade always within reach.

In addition to that, it comes integrated with a Bluetooth function for fast and wireless cutting. Therefore, you can connect the machine to your tablet, desktop, or smartphone and control it without the need for cables or wires. You can also send all your crafts and projects wirelessly to the device for cutting. On top of that, the device is fitted with the easy-to-use Design Space software that is compatible with nearly all Android and iOS devices, and Mac and Windows computers. The software enables you to access thousands of fonts and images for free or at a small fee.

Further, the Explore Air includes the popular Smart Set dial function to help you make intricate cuts or create custom settings for various materials. Thanks to its Cut Smart technology, making clean cuts of all sorts of sizes and shapes is also easy.

Pros

- Cuts and writes in just a single step
- Well-made with durable blades, easy to set up and use
- Supports cartridges
- Super convenient and easy to use the iPad app
- Includes orange grid-lines to ensure designs stay centered
- Supports wireless cutting

Cons

- Only works if there is an internet connection
- Design software is a bit slow

Cricut Explore Air 2

Next up we have the Explore Air 2 that is reported to be two times faster than the previous Explore models. From home decor to cards and custom t-shirts, the machine allows you to create stunning DIY projects in just minutes. On top of that, it cuts over 100 types of materials such as specialty paper, Iron-on Vinyls, faux leather, poster board, cardstock, adhesive foils, and more.

The Explore Air 2, like the Explore One and Air, makes intricate cuts every time thanks to its Smart Set Dial function. This function allows the machine to create cuts only at the correct pressure and depth for all kinds of materials. In addition to this, it includes the free Design Space software that is cloud-based. The software enables you to edit and customize your projects on the go.

What is more, it features a dual tool holder so you can cut and write or simply cut and score in a single step. Using the Cricut pens, you can make handwritten cards or projects using your favorite font for free. Also, you can easily create fold lines for boxes, cards, paper crafts, and envelopes using a scoring stylus. Another feature worth mentioning is its built-in Bluetooth connectivity designed to ensure faster wireless cutting, scoring, and writing. Consequently, you can send your designs and projects from your smartphone, computer, or tablet to the machine for optimal convenience.

With over 3,000 pre-made projects and design ideas to choose from, the machine provides you with endless possibilities in the image library. Besides, you can always upload and use your image files, artwork as well as fonts absolutely for free. As if that's not enough, the Explore Air 2 enables you to print full-color patterns or images and then cut them out.

Pros

- Cuts easily through printable images
- Easy-to-use software
- Cuts and writes up-to 2X faster
- Includes images and thousands of design ideas for nearly every project
- Boasts easy material settings
- Beautiful and stylish design with vintage colors

Cons

- ❖ Some users have has issues with the software
- ❖ Cutting mat loses its sticky very fast

CONCLUSION

Learning to use the Cricut Explore Air 2 can be hard. For absolute beginners, the machine can easily come off as overwhelming. There is also a long learning curve involved. I know this because I went through that learning curve. I have therefore written this book detailing my experience with the Cricut Explore Air 2 and providing an easy to follow guide so that you can get somewhat of a short cut to mastering the machine. With this book in hand, you no longer have to go through the long learning curve I went through. All you have to do is hold my hands as I guide you.

Inside you will find step by step instructions that will help you master Cricut Explore Air 2. Starting from how to correctly set up your machine, this book will teach you how to use your Cricut Explore Air 2 to create T-shirt designs, design bracelets, paper arts, and stickers; make beautiful designs on fabrics, troubleshot your machine, and a whole lot more. Also, you will find a complete step by step guide on how to set up Cricut Design Space, how to work with text, images, and bookmarks in the Cricut design space; together with cutting instructions for various materials. Cricut machines might be useful for various tasks. Their versatility and effectiveness are making them popular options when it comes to die-cutting. That is why you need a Cricut machine, particularly when you're a skilled crafter. If you're a newbie, the best cutting machine for you will be the multi-featured one and is easy to use.

What you stand to learn from this book: -How to Set Up Your Cricut Machine-How to Cut Heavyweight and Lightweight Materials-Working with Fonts in the Design Space-How to Use Images in Cricut Design Space-How to Clean the Cricut Machine-Troubleshooting Your Cricut Explore Air Machine-Tips on How to Use the Cricut Explore Air Effectively-How to Make a Customized Graphic T-Shirt-Making money with Cricut-How to Make Stickers with Cricut-How to Make DIY Paper Succulent with Your Cricut-How to Make Fabric Bookmark Using Your Cricut Machine?-How to Make a Frosty Wreath?-How to Make Faux Leather Bracelet -How to Make Planner Stickers with Cricut-And a lot more.

CPSIA information can be obtained
at www.ICGtesting.com
Printed in the USA
BVHW040741060221
599449BV00006B/51

9 781914 346088